FORERUNNERS: IDEAS FIRST
FROM THE UNIVERSITY OF MINNESOTA PRESS

Original e-works to spark new scholarship

FORERUNNERS: IDEAS FIRST is a thought-in-process series of break-through digital works. Written between fresh ideas and finished books, Forerunners draws on scholarly work initiated in notable blogs, social media, conference plenaries, journal articles, and the synergy of academic exchange. This is gray literature publishing: where intense thinking, change, and speculation take place in scholarship.

Fifty Years of *The Battle of Algiers*

Fifty Years of
The Battle of Algiers
Past as Prologue

Sohail Daulatzai

University of Minnesota Press

MINNEAPOLIS

Portions of "Third World Dreams," "Fanon as Prophet, Algeria as
Revolutionary Mecca," and "The Camera as Gun" were published in
*Black Star, Crescent Moon: The Muslim International and Black Freedom
beyond America* (Minneapolis: University of Minnesota Press, 2012).

Published by the University of Minnesota Press
111 Third Avenue South, Suite 290
Minneapolis, MN 55401-2520

The University of Minnesota is an equal-opportunity educator and
employer.

From the wreckage we declare our name:

Je Suis Ali La Pointe

Contents

Introduction: Fifty Years of the Boomerang

THE BATTLE OF ALGIERS IS STILL BEING WAGED, only now on a planetary scale. Everywhere the unrest is permanent, and everywhere the war declared on it is perpetual. Gaza. Ayotzinapa. Compton. Lagos. The world is a crime scene, with borders drawn in chalk outline. Security and order define and refine statecraft, resurrecting the unruly as the specter and threat to peace and stability. Police forces have proliferated. Brussels and Paris have been locked down. So too was Boston. Baghdad and Kabul are the laboratories; so too was Detroit. The threat perception is amorphous, boundless, everywhere, mirroring and mandated by the necropolitics of racial capital. The checkpoint is mobile and the barbed wire is ambient, while the guillotine looms. Counterinsurgency is the strategy and the tactic. The Law is an inconvenience and ethics a mere contrivance. House-to-house sweeps, gang injunctions, militarized borders, stop and frisks, surveillance aircraft, drone-fare, torture, indefinite detention, targeted assassinations: these are the predicates for liberal democracy and the protection of white life. The state of exception is the rule.

Though *The Battle of Algiers* (dir. Gillo Pontecorvo, 1966) was made fifty years ago, it's as if it never ended. From the corridors of power to the tunnels of Gaza, we are seemingly still living the film. Only now it's being billed as the "War on Terror," a sequel to another prequel that is part horror, part absurdist drama, and part dystopic sci-fi, where mosques have become morgues and killing fields turned to theme parks. The names of the droned, tortured, and maimed can't even be mentioned. And if they are, they're mispronounced. Amid the carnage, some wield the dialectic and others the gun, while the hunt for Ali La Pointe continues . . .

Prior to the invasion of Iraq in 2003, the largest antiwar protest in history took place throughout the world. But to no avail. President Bush dismissed the protestors as "a focus group," unleashing the bombing campaign that was known as "Shock and Awe." Soon after the invasion, in late 2003, the Pentagon invited the military brass to a screening of *The Battle of Algiers,* and the teaser read,

> How to win a battle against terrorism and lose the war of ideas. Children shoot soldiers at point-blank range. Women plant bombs in cafes. Soon the entire Arab population builds to a mad fervor. Sound familiar? The French have a plan. It succeeds tactically, but fails strategically. To understand why, come to a rare showing of this film.[1]

Re-released by Criterion DVD Collections shortly after the Pentagon screening, including a theatrical run as well, *The Battle of Algiers* is widely considered the greatest political film of all time, having won numerous prestigious international awards, including being nominated for three Oscars. It is mentioned by filmmakers as diverse as Mira Nair, Paul Greengrass, Spike Lee, Steven Soderbergh, Oliver Stone, and Julian Schnabel, among others, as being deeply influential on their own work. But the resurgence of the film in the post-9/11 context has been both troubling and telling.

In addition to the Pentagon screening, the film was mentioned in a congressional hearing titled "Preparing for the War on Terrorism" just nine days after 9/11. In speaking about "al-

1. Michael T. Kaufman, "The World: Film Studies; What Does the Pentagon See in 'Battle of Algiers?,'" *New York Times,* September 7, 2003. http://www.nytimes.com/2003/09/07/weekinreview/the-world-film-studies-what-does-the-pentagon-see-in-battle-of-algiers.html.

Qaeda," Christopher Harmon, a professor at the U.S. Marine Corps Command and Staff College, would claim, "They use a cell structure that has never been better explained publicly than in the famous film *The Battle of Algiers* . . . in which a clandestine organization can form and operate and, while never impenetrable, reduce some of its counterintelligence problems."[2]

Also, Richard Clarke, the doyen of the national security establishment, who worked for Presidents Reagan, George H. W. Bush, Clinton, and George W. Bush in various high-level capacities, including as chief advisor on the National Security Council from 1998 to 2003, would come to prominence as the "critical" voice in the political class after leaving the George W. Bush inner circle. In expressing his disagreement with the approach to "counterterrorism" under the Bush–Cheney junta, Clarke argued that the attacks shown in *The Battle of Algiers* "may have been the 1950's, but it's all happening now in the 21st century."[3]

In presenting a world violently defined by colonialism, only to then shatter that world's seeming invincibility with a defiance that was at once shocking and gut wrenching, *The Battle of Algiers* gave voice and dignity to Algerian resistance to French colonial occupation. What interest would the Pentagon have in the film? How could a film that was so sympathetic to the Algerians—evocatively and poetically showing them organizing, targeting French occupation forces, and planting bombs in cafés and other public places—come to the service of the most powerful empire in the history of the world fifty years after it was released? And why did the Algerian War have such an impact on post-9/11 U.S. military policy, so much so that the Petraeus Doctrine—the blueprint

2. U.S. Congress, House of Representatives, Committee on Government Reform, *Preparing for the War on Terror: Hearings before the Committee on Government Reform,* 107th Cong., 1st sess. (2001), 112.

3. Richard A. Clarke, Christopher E. Isham, and Michael A. Sheehan, "The Battle of Algiers: A Case Study," produced by Abbey Lustgarten and Kim Hendrickson, disc 3, *The Battle of Algiers,* directed by Gillo Pontecorvo (1966; New York: The Criterion Collection, 2004), special ed. DVD.

for U.S. counterinsurgency in Iraq, Afghanistan, and elsewhere—was deeply indebted to French military specialist David Galula's books *Pacification in Algeria* and *Counterinsurgency Warfare*?

The Battle of Algiers is an itinerant film, a nomadic text that has migrated throughout the world and has, echoing Edward Said's "traveling theory," been embraced by a diverse group of revolutionaries, rebel groups, and leftists as well as revanchist, right-wing dictators, military juntas, and imperial war machines. The film has always been a battleground for competing ideas about power and politics at different historical junctures and in varying places around the globe. In fact, part of the film's impact comes from the diverse sympathies it has engendered and the sheer range of interests that have identified with the film from across the political spectrum, whether it be in the favelas of Brazil or on the front lines of the Palestine Liberation Organization, the Tamil Tigers, the Irish Republican Army (IRA), or Black Power; from the war rooms of the Pentagon to the courtrooms of the Panther 21 trial; from the factory floors in Iran to the palaces where Dirty Wars were planned; and from community centers in Los Angeles to art house theaters in Havana, Mexico City, and Montevideo.

Fifty years on, tracing the roots and routes of *The Battle of Algiers* gives us a panoramic view of the massive global upheavals of the last half-century, where formal European colonies crumbled, the United States rose to leviathan status, and imperial control reconstituted itself in the face of Third World liberation struggles and Black freedom movements. This book situates the roots of this film within the era of decolonization, revolutionary struggle, and the emergence of Third Cinema. But in also mapping the routes the film traveled, this book tells the enduring story of how a larger tapestry of resistance to the legacies of slavery and colonialism took shape throughout the world in different historical contexts, while also revealing how the networks of repression tried to silence and crush those movements to maintain their violent rule.

By exploring the film's production and reception history, as well as its uses and meanings during the rising tide of decolonization and its aftermath, this book will detail the aesthetic dimensions and political contexts of the film, including the countries where it was banned, the regimes that screened it for counterinsurgency purposes, and the organizations and movements that embraced it as a template and inspiration for resistance.

But unlike traditional film scholarship, this is not the conventional book that would celebrate the fiftieth anniversary of a film solely by detailing its production and reception history and the historical and political contexts in which it was made. Instead, this book marks the fifty years since the film's release to reveal that *The Battle of Algiers* is more than an artifact or relic of the past; it is a prescient and telling testament to the present.

The screening of the film at the Pentagon and the racial logic of the "War on Terror" have sought to control the memory of *The Battle of Algiers* and, at the same time, have negated the central questions and concerns that decolonization and the Third World Project sought to address: structural global inequality; wealth and resource exploitation of the non-Western world; continual foreign intervention into and destabilization of the Third World; and deeply entrenched asymmetries in diplomatic, political, and economic power between the West and the Global South. It is these structural violences that now sit at the heart of the "War on Terror," and it is their systematic silencing of which *The Battle of Algiers* continues to be a haunting reminder.

There is no more clairvoyant a voice about the ravages of colonialism, the necessity of decolonization, and the entanglements of its aftermath than Frantz Fanon. As a psychiatrist, revolutionary, and theorist, Fanon spent a great deal of time in Algeria, using his experiences there and his sympathies for the Algerian cause as the basis for most of his writing and his revolutionary activities. Fanon has been arguably the most influential thinker on race and colonialism, and his masterpiece *The Wretched of the Earth* (1961) would become his most famous work. In many ways, *The Battle of Algiers* is the cinematic embodiment of *Wretched*, which explored the poetics of armed struggle, the segregation of colonial space, the creation of a new national consciousness, the impact of colonial torture, and his critiques of and warnings about an indigenous national bourgeoisie who would betray the popular will.

Prophetically and tragically, many of Fanon's warnings and insights came true, as the legacies of colonialism and Western domination still structure an unequal world. *The Battle of Algiers*'s relevance throughout the last fifty years endures not despite the violence and domination that continue to sit at the core of the global order but because of it—the film a haunting of the imperial consensus that today has declared a "War on Terror" so as to shield and even erase the means through which the legacies of colonialism and slavery continue to operate. Precisely because of this, I'm suggesting that *The Battle of Algiers* is the paradigmatic text for understanding the post-9/11 world that we now inhabit, one where the threat of the Muslim looms, serving as an avatar for the rewriting of the colonial past and the fortifying of the imperial present.

Specters of the Muslim

The "War on Terror" has been made possible because the racial panic of the "Muslim threat" has generated tremendous ideological capital and political will. The National Defense Authorization Act (2012) has declared that "the world is a battlefield," echoing the *9/11 Commission Report* (2004) that referred to the "American homeland as the planet." Both documents have given sanction and staked a claim to the necessity of full-spectrum dominance and U.S. dominion over the globe, an imperial form of governance made manifest through the declaration of perpetual war, the normalization of torture, the use of targeted assassinations, indefinite detentions, the emergence of Guantánamo and other CIA "black sites," military tribunals, and other legal regimes of expendability and violence.

What has been the edifice and scaffolding for the current imperial posture has been the policy of "antiterrorism," a racial logic in which "terrorism" (or "terrorist") is a twenty-first-century way of marking the savage and of invoking the colonial binary of "civilization" and "savagery." This has become a coded way of constructing race and Otherness, as the logic of "terror" (like "savage" before it) exorcises particular ideas, bodies, regions, and collectives from the category of the human (i.e., whiteness) and the political community of rights. Occupying what Fanon called the "zone of non-being," Islam and Muslims, then, are understood as outside the category of modernity, seen as irrational, savage, and uncivilized. And because they are outside the community of the human, Muslims are not sovereign, nor are they rights bearing, and so they are not subject to the protections that those deemed modern citizen-subjects have from violence, war, containment, and so on. As a result, the Muslim then becomes the embodiment of the limits of the political, occupying a Fanonian zone in which they must be contained or killed to protect the rights of all others (i.e., those deemed human) because Muslims are seen as fundamental threats to democracy, freedom, women, and Western values and norms. In fact, Muslims are presumed guilty, and only deemed not so after their death. One example of this is U.S. drone policy that deems any military -age Muslim male within a strike zone to be a combatant who, when killed, can only be deemed "innocent" posthumously, and only if explicit evidence can be shown to prove him so.

These rationales have resulted in the deaths of almost 2 million people in the two declared wars in Afghanistan and Iraq, not to mention the U.S.-led invasion of Libya and the assassination of Muammar Gaddafi; the U.S.-backed Saudi war against Yemen; intervention and escalation in Syria; drone bombings in Pakistan, Yemen, and Somalia; the deepening of a U.S. imperial footprint in Africa via the U.S. Africa Command (AFRICOM); the further destabilization of Latin America; the maintenance of U.S.-backed gulf monarchies and other client states; and the material and diplomatic support of Zionist dispossession of Palestinian lands.

On the domestic front, the "Muslim threat" has been predicated on the stoking of white supremacy as an organizing principle around "security," resulting in a fundamental restructuring of the federal government with the creation of the Department of Homeland Security, the passage of the USA PATRIOT Act, the creation of a massive surveillance architecture, the ratcheting up of police power and other militarized forces that further target Black and Brown communities, the proliferation of detention camps, fundamental assaults on any vestige of legal redress, and curtailment and eradication of political dissent.

More specifically, the "Muslim threat" has reignited fears of a "creeping Sharia law" and the threats that Islam poses to American pluralism. This has resulted in calling for the further policing of Muslim mobility and movement, from a complete ban on Muslim immigration to stepping up Muslim deportations, the calls for use of special IDs and special registration for Muslims, and even the invoking of internment camps, as was the case for the Japanese in World War II. And though there is concern about warrantless wiretapping on citizens, there is widespread support for surveillance of those deemed "suspicious" (i.e., Muslims) as well as calls for stepping up policies already in place that patrol and infiltrate Muslim student groups, places of worship, shopping areas, and community gatherings. In addition, congressional hearings on "radicalization" and federal programs such as "Countering-Violent Extremism" continue to target and racialize Muslim communities and further embolden police powers.

Outside of the United States, throughout Europe, Canada, and Australia, the specter of the Muslim has united neoliberals and social democrats, Marxist Leftists and conservative Christians, feminists and anarchists. Presidents and prime ministers throughout the European Union have catered to and reinvigorated a deeply anti-Muslim discourse, stoking fears of rape, criminality, "terror," and security as well as "cultural" fears about undermining white Christian European identity and values. British prime minister David Cameron and German chancellor Angela Merkel declared the end of multiculturalism due to the threat of "Islamism" and the presence of Muslims within their borders, as liberal, center, and far -right fears have been stoked throughout the continent, resulting in the rise of right-wing nationalist groups, anti-immigrant initiatives, calls for turning back refugees and closing borders, violent attacks on Muslims, and the empowerment of security and police forces throughout Europe. In France, where the Muslim veil has been banned, Charlie Hebdo and the attacks in France made "free speech" yet another pillar of the West supposedly under assault, as "Je Suis Charlie" became a slogan for the erasure not only of the French colonial past in Algeria and elsewhere but also of the larger Western colonial project and its legacy in the imperial present. Liberal and leftist philosophers and academics have also joined the fray: Derrida asserts that "Islam is the Other of democracy," while Žižek has relied on Eurocentric tropes about "values" in relation to Muslim migrants, while also claiming that, in Islam, "there is the inexistence of the feminine."[4]

As the threat of the Muslim looms, defining Western statecraft, and haunting the tattered edges of modernity, *The Battle of Algiers* serves as a diagnostic, a parable, or even an allegory of the moment. By exploring the film and its afterlives, as well as the debates it engaged around revolutionary violence, gender and the role of women, torture, and the postindependence moment, this book restages *The Battle of Algiers* for our current time, asking how it can be a resource or archive to think through the social life of the "War on Terror" and how the current U.S. imperial posture has continued a decades-long, and even centuries-long, project to decimate and undermine much of the global Left.

The film's embrace over the last fifty years by a diverse group of leftists and revolutionaries speaks to its broad appeal, a kind of radical universality in which the film was only nominally, and

4. Jacques Derrida and Slavoj Žižek, quoted in Anne Norton, *On the Muslim Question* (Princeton, N.J.: Princeton University Press, 2013), 46, 119.

incidentally, about Muslims. But in a post-9/11 context, a troubling inversion has occurred that attempts to undermine the film and its politics: the very universality that gave the film its power has been stripped away and replaced by a narrower reading that this is a film specifically about Muslims who are not just resisting French (read Western) occupation but a film that *celebrated* Muslim resistance. And in the context of the "War on Terror," where the space for Muslim subjectivity has been obliterated, armed struggle, or resistance of *any* kind, by Muslims is not only not palatable but seen as threatening and worthy of death.

This framing of the film through the present holds the danger of suggesting that sympathy and identification with Muslims resisting is not only dangerous but also politically and ethically baseless, fracturing the very kinds of solidarities and alliances that are vital to challenging the current structures of power that are rooted in deep histories of slavery and colonization. The framing of the film through the "War on Terror" also sanitizes and rewrites the colonial past so that Algerian resistance is delegitimized and French colonialism is redeemed through the contemporary "War on Terror." But not just the past—the current project of empire, the invasions of Iraq and Afghanistan, and the machinery of violence are also coded as innocent and just, where the French of yesterday are the Americans of today. But if that's the case, that the Americans of today see themselves as the French of yesterday, the Algerians, then, are Palestinians, Afghans, Zapatistas, Black Lives Matter activists, and all those who live in favelas, banlieues, townships, ghettos, barrios, and refugee camps. To watch *The Battle of Algiers* and see yourself in Hassiba, Ali, or Omar is to reclaim a radical legacy—and is an insurrectionary act.

The Battle of Algiers offers up that potential of insurgent possibility, a utopian demand in today's climate where authoritarianism is the rule, history has seemingly ended, and politics have been emptied. The film's poetry imagines that authority can be challenged, that dignity is possible, that freedom and the quest for it are not anachronistic—and that in the "War on Terror," with perpetual war, massive surveillance, economic dispossession, and racist rule, the memory of a global struggle against larger, seemingly more powerful forces is not only vital but devastatingly urgent.

Past

Third World Dreams

THE BATTLE OF ALGIERS marked a paradigm shift in film art, deeply influencing what came to be known as Third Cinema, a cinematic movement that emerged during the period of decolonization in the Third World. Seeking to wed film art and production to popular people's struggles by challenging dominant cinematic practices, *The Battle of Algiers* was striking, as its aesthetic and formal techniques forced spectators and filmmakers alike to reimagine the possibilities of cinema. The defiant ambition shown by the Algerians on the streets was matched by the boldness of the aesthetic choices on-screen. A fiery combination of form and content, *The Battle of Algiers*—like its political arm of decolonization—sought to strip away the veneer and artifice of dominant cinematic style, a move at once aesthetic and ideological, one that suggested that film could either mask the realities of inequality and injustice in the world or lay bare their root causes and suggest possible solutions.

Though the film centered on the defeat of the Algerian National Liberation Front (FLN) in the actual Battle of Algiers that took place from 1954 to 1957, it ended on the victory of the Algerian people as the new nation was born in 1962. The Algerian struggle for independence was itself part of a larger global, interconnected, anticolonial struggle being waged after World War II, an era of tremendous turmoil and upheaval that continues to have an enduring impact today. Contrary to the conventional narrative about the "Great War," which is framed as a struggle between the forces of Nazism and fascism (Germany, Italy, and Japan) against those of democracy and freedom (the United States, France, and Britain), World War II was a more complicated, and in many ways more simple, affair, revealing as it did the deep contradictions within liberal modernity and its notions of freedom.

The anticolonial thinker and surrealist poet Aimé Césaire's masterpiece *Discourse on Colonialism* laid bare the hypocrisy within the West around World War II. To Césaire, there was no difference between the Nazism of Hitler and the colonialism of the British and French empires—both were rooted in a master race philosophy of white supremacy. To many, the struggle between the Axis and Allies was not one between forces of fascism and forces of freedom, as is conventionally told. It was in effect about European control of the Third World. As payback for the decimation of Germany in World War I, Hitler wanted what the British and French had—their colonies and the wealth that they produced.

For Césaire, the British and the French were only upset at Hitler because he inflicted upon them what the British and French had been doing to the Third World with impunity for centuries. According to Césaire, before the British and the French were victims of Nazism, "they were its accomplices; that they tolerated that Nazism before it was inflicted upon them, that they absolved it, shut their eyes to it, legitimized it."[1] Césaire would go on to say that Nazism has engulfed "the whole of Western, Christian civilization in its reddened waters" and that the Western European "has a Hitler inside him, that Hitler inhabits him," and that what he cannot forgive Hitler for is not "the crime in itself, the crime against man . . . it is the crime against the white man, the humiliation of the white man, and the fact that he [Hitler] applied to

---

1. Aimé Césaire, *Discourse on Colonialism,* trans. Joan Pinkham (1955; repr., New York: Monthly Review Press, 2000), 36.

Europe colonialist procedures which until then had been reserved exclusively for the Arabs of Algeria, the 'coolies' of India, and the 'niggers' of Africa."[2] Césaire powerfully captured what many in the Third World had experienced so viscerally and so violently: that colonialism and Nazi fascism were kindred spirits, natural allies and outgrowths of a European modernity that cast the darker world outside the category of the human, and therefore of rights, legitimacy, and self-determination.

The hypocrisies ran deep. But despite them, the French and the British asked, implored, and even demanded that their colonial subjects fight to protect the French Republic and the British Crown from Hitler. Contrary to popular belief, the French and the British did not fight the war; their empires did. Millions of colonial subjects fought in the war, including Frantz Fanon, in what is largely an untold story as they faced tremendous racism within the ranks of the British and French armies, as can be seen in films like Ousmane Sembene's *Camp de Thiaroye* (1988) and Rachid Bouchareb's *Days of Glory* (2006). And they were vital to the defeat of Hitler. But many also did not fight, unwilling as they were to participate in what they saw as a ruse. Black soldiers who fought for the United States experienced something similar. Not only were they treated as inferior by their own white U.S. compatriots—subject to harassment and violence as well as vastly disproportionate exposure to lethal, toxic chemical weapons—but German POWs were able to eat in the same mess halls as white U.S. soldiers, while Black soldiers were segregated.

Those who did fight did so with certain promises from the British and the French. Because the war was about "freedom" and "democracy," the colonies demanded the same for themselves, using these as principled levers to hold the colonial powers to their word. If the war was about making the world safe for democracy, freedom, and self-determination, then what about the Third World? Didn't European colonialism prevent the people of Africa,

2. Ibid.

Asia, and Latin America from achieving these universal ideals, and didn't they also deserve the possibility of shaping their own destiny free from tyranny?

Apparently not. With the end of the war, just as for the Black soldiers who returned to the United States and saw that the master race philosophy was alive and well through the racial violence of legally sanctioned Jim Crow, lynchings, and brutally enforced segregation in housing, education, and transportation, many of the promises given by the British and the French toward their colonial subjects who fought were reneged upon as well.

In the aftermath of the war, the United States emerged as the global power, an empire with its own histories of slavery, native genocide, and imperial expansion. The United States sought to underwrite European colonialism by bolstering the British and French under the Marshall Plan and the Atlantic Charter. Using the Cold War logic that communism was a bigger threat to the Third World than colonialism, the United States gave massive aid to help rebuild Europe and, in effect, strengthen the British and French holds on their colonies in the aftermath of the war. This of course was done under the watchful eye of the Third World and to the vehement protest of W. E. B. Du Bois, Paul Robeson, and the rest of the Black Left in the United States, who found common cause with the people of Africa, Asia, and Latin America.

For the Algerians in particular, the end of the war was a moment to galvanize a national consciousness to challenge French rule and hold the French to their word regarding democracy and self-determination. On May 8, 1945, thousands of Algerians used the occasion of German surrender, known as V-E Day (for "Victory in Europe"), to march, demanding freedom in the eastern Algerian city of Sétif. As the sounds of cheering crowds echoed throughout Europe and the United States that day, the staccato sound of gunfire rang throughout Sétif as an estimated forty-five thousand Algerians were massacred over several days to crush their nationalist hopes. The echoes of Setif reverberated throughout the Third World, and though many trace the formal beginning of the

Algerian War of Independence to November 1, 1954, it was in Sétif where the seeds of the modern uprising were planted.

It's not surprising that many French officers who fought to maintain colonialism in Vietnam, Algeria, and elsewhere were Nazi collaborators during the German occupation of France under the Vichy regime. These included Maurice Papon, who, as chief of the Paris police, was responsible for the brutal torture of Algerians in France, including the killing of more than two hundred Algerian protestors and the disappearances of hundreds more in Paris in October 1961 during the Algerian War—which still stands as the largest massacre on European soil in history.[3] But even those who were part of the glorified French Resistance to Hitler—like Colonel Matthieu in *The Battle of Algiers*—fought to maintain colonialism, the point being that whether one was a Nazi sympathizer or a French "humanist," maintaining the empire and control over the Third World remained central to a white worldview and the West's collective sense of self.

These contradictions and hypocrisies that Césaire laid bare—and that came to be embodied in Sétif and every liberation struggle after it—are still the scandal that haunts the West. It is an open secret that racial domination of the Global South continues, despite the rhetoric and language of democracy, independence, and self-governance. The revolutionary struggles that emerged after World War II in both the Third World and by Black radical movements in the United States were precisely about addressing the tensions that Césaire laid out about the failures of modernity and its exclusionary notions of rights and equality. As a result, this created a tremendous sense of solidarity and shared struggle against European and U.S. power from the nonwhite world, a racial internationalism that would fundamentally shape what came to be known as the Third World Project through gatherings, organizations, artistic and cultural networks, military training

3. *Drowning by Bullets,* directed by Philip Brooks and Alan Hayling (1992; Brooklyn, N.Y.: Icarus Films, 2003), DVD.

and weapons support, and diplomatic and political channels that were established to try to create a new and more just global order.

The Bandung Conference of 1955 was one example. As the national liberation movements were gaining momentum throughout the world in the aftermath of World War II, leaders such as Kwame Nkrumah of Ghana, Fidel Castro of Cuba, Ahmed Ben Bella of Algeria, and Gamal Abdel Nasser of Egypt came into global consciousness as a result of their strident critiques of colonialism and its cancerous corollary: white supremacy. This kind of global racial consciousness led to the 1955 Asian–African Conference in Bandung, Indonesia, where twenty-nine countries from Africa and Asia converged to renounce both white supremacy and the false choice—between the United States and the Soviet Union—being offered to newly liberated countries throughout the world. As a clear challenge to white world supremacy and American–Soviet dominance, these countries participating at Bandung created a defiant platform of resistance that resonated throughout the Third World.

The 1955 Afro-Asian Conference in Bandung was arguably the most important international gathering of the century, one with incredible implications not only for the Third World, Europe, and the Cold War but also for Black peoples in the United States. Occurring just ten years after the end of World War II and amid tremendous political upheaval, the twenty-nine countries that Bandung brought together represented half of the world's population at the time.

At the opening address of the conference, Indonesian president Ahmed Sukarno captured the hopeful tone in his speech, "Let a New Asia and a New Africa Be Born," when he declared that "the nations of Asia and Africa are no longer the tools and playthings" of Europe, the United States, or the Soviets. Bandung was more than a shot across the bow at the powerful; it was a gathering that held the promise of a radically different world order from the centuries of white power, colonialism, and capitalist control of almost the entire globe. And so it's no surprise that the conference and the implications it held became a battleground upon which questions of sovereignty, white supremacy, and nationalism would unfold. In fact, Bandung challenged the white world, foregrounding the role of race within global affairs.[4]

Following Bandung's example, the spirit of Third Worldism as a project began to take shape as anticolonial struggles and international solidarity among the oppressed rocked the colonial order. The Afro-Asian Peoples Solidarity Organization, which was the follow-up to Bandung, met in Cairo in 1957. That same year, Kwame Nkrumah led Ghana to independence from Britain, while the following year saw Ahmed Sékou Touré declare Guinean independence, the only African colony at the time to reject France's desire to remain "interdependent" under what de Gaulle called the "French Community." In 1958, Abd al-Karim Qasim overthrew the British- and U.S.-backed Hashemite monarchy in Iraq and then proceeded to break from the pro-Western Baghdad Pact, while Nasser created the United Arab Republic (which included Egypt and Syria) as a means to forge a larger pan-Arab state. In 1959, ninety miles from the United States, Fidel Castro and his guerilla army overthrew the U.S.-backed dictator Fulgencio Batista and liberated Cuba, sending shock waves throughout the Yankee establishment and forever changing the landscape of anti-imperial struggle throughout Latin America and the Global South. One year later, fourteen African nations would gain independence, including the Congo, which was led by the charismatic Patrice Lumumba. And in 1961, the Non-Aligned Movement was born in Belgrade as a means of crafting an alternative path for newly independent countries outside of the orbit of the U.S.–Soviet Cold War.

The spirit of radical internationalism against the old order would continue, and 1966 was a seminal year. Not only was *The*

---

4. Sohail Daulatzai, *Black Star, Crescent Moon: The Muslim International and Black Freedom beyond America* (Minneapolis: University of Minnesota Press, 2012).

Battle of Algiers released but it was also the year that the Black Panther Party was founded by Huey Newton and Bobby Seale in Oakland, California. As part of the global struggles against colonialism and white supremacy, the Tricontinental Conference also took place in 1966 in Havana, Cuba. Calling itself the Organization of Solidarity of the People of Africa, Asia, and Latin America (OSPAAAL), it became a vital force of solidarity for the Third World. Taking a more militant stand than the Non-Aligned Movement did against the Cold War binary of the United States and the Soviet Union, *tricontinentalism* (as it came to be known) also took Bandung's charge and extended international solidarity to include Latin America and also Black, Brown, and other communities struggling against white supremacy in the United States. As part of their project, they produced news bulletins, essays, interviews, speeches, and analysis of liberation struggles throughout the Third World, as well as political graphic poster art that expressed solidarity with global struggles against imperialism taking place in Africa and Asia and throughout the Americas.[5]

These global dynamics led to the emergence of a distinctly Third World Left within U.S.-based Black communities that began to emerge in the 1950s and continued on during the mid- to late 1960s and early 1970s. This influence was undeniable, especially in light of the vocabulary that Malcolm X, Robert Williams, Harold Cruse, and numerous others crafted in the 1950s and 1960s, situating Black struggles in the United States alongside and in solidarity with the struggles of the peoples of the Third World.

This spirit of internationalism was what defined Malcolm X and his political project that challenged Euro-American power, claiming "it has been since the Bandung Conference that all dark people on the earth have been striding towards freedom . . .

5. Anne Garland Mahler, "The Global South in the Belly of the Beast: Viewing African American Civil Rights through a Tricontinental Lens," *Latin American Research Review* 50, no. 1 (2015): 95–116.

At Bandung they had to agree that as long as they remained divided a handful of whites would continue to rule them. But once our African [and] Asian brothers put their religious and political differences into the background, their unity has had sufficient force to break the bonds of colonialism, imperialism, Europeanism . . . which are all only diplomatic terms for the same thing, white supremacy." Patrice Lumumba, whom Malcolm X called the "greatest Black man who ever walked the African continent," was elected as the first Prime Minister of the Congo in 1960. But within ten weeks of being elected, Lumumba was kidnapped, imprisoned, and brutally murdered by the CIA. While in prison, Lumumba would write in his last letter: "We are not alone. Africa, Asia, and free and liberated peoples in every corner of the globe will ever remain at the side of the millions of Congolese."[6]

With the Black Panthers vocally supporting the National Liberation Front (NLF) of Vietnam and even offering up Black men to fight as soldiers in the NLF against the U.S. military, and with the influence of Che Guevara, Mao Tse-tung, Frantz Fanon, Patrice Lumumba, the Mau Mau of Kenya, and the Third World anticolonialism of Cuba, Algeria, and China, the militancy of the moment saw kindred souls in the national liberation struggles taking place throughout Africa and Asia. The "revolutionary violence" of Guevara, Fanon, and others captured the hearts and minds of young Black radicals in the streets, as the Revolutionary Action Movement (RAM), the Black Panthers, and other radical youth within Puerto Rican, Native American, Chicano, and Asian communities formed groups such as the Young Lords Party, the American Indian Movement, the Brown Berets, and I Wor Kuen. The spirit of internationalism was endemic and widespread in the United States through the use of the Third World and colonialism as lenses to frame and understand the conditions of Black peoples in the United States. As

6. Daulatzai, *Black Star, Crescent Moon*, 161.

Stokely Carmichael said, "Black Power means that we see ourselves as part of the Third World; that we see our struggle as closely related to liberation struggle around the world."[7]

And he was far from the exception. Black Panther Party member Kathleen Cleaver said, "From its inception, the Black Panther Party saw the condition of Blacks in an international context, recognizing that the same racist imperialism that people in Africa, Asia, Latin America were fighting against was victimizing Blacks in the United States." Robert Williams, whose book *Negroes with Guns* advocated for armed self-defense and resistance on the part of Black people in the South, had a profound influence on Black radicals and became a lightning rod for controversy in the late 1950s. Forced to flee to Cuba and then to China after being framed for kidnapping in the United States, Williams said, "I'm interested in the problems of Africa, Asia and Latin America. I believe that we all have the same struggle, a struggle for liberation." In addition, Harold Cruse had said, "What is true of the colonial world is also true of the Negro in the United States," and Max Stanford of the RAM saw Black peoples in the United States as part of the Bandung world of Africa, Asia, and Latin America. Stanford (who later converted to Islam and became Muhammad Ahmad) was deeply inspired by Malcolm X and Robert Williams, and he organized conferences and wrote articles about the Black revolution's links to the Third World, his "Bandung Humanism" becoming the rubric and central theme for defining Black politics and solidarities with national liberation struggles taking place in Cuba, Algeria, Vietnam, China, and elsewhere.[8]

The kinds of international solidarities and global alliances that were forged around decolonization and national liberation struggles throughout the 1950s, 1960s, and 1970s gave shape to what has been referred to as "Third Worldism," fundamentally challenging the global order. Having just fought a successful but brutal

7. Ibid., 47.
8. Ibid., 47–48.

anticolonial war against the French that captured the hearts and minds of revolutionaries in both the Third World and the United States, Algeria's independence struggle was being waged within this crucible, and it profoundly shaped the nationalist struggle and its relationship to Third Worldism. During and after its liberation war, Algeria would became a flashpoint for revolutionary internationalism connecting Senegal to Sudan, Palestine to South Africa, Oakland to Algiers, and Black peoples in the United States to the Third World.

Fanon as Prophet,
Algeria as Revolutionary Mecca

INFLUENCING GUERRILLAS, artists, and intellectuals in the United States, Latin America, Africa, the Middle East, South Asia, and beyond, Frantz Fanon became synonymous with the righteous indignation of the Third World in response to European and U.S. power. Fanon's influence came not only because he was closely linked with the Algerian anticolonial movement but also because he was seen as the voice and theorist for revolutionary violence, national liberation, and Third World solidarity.

His analysis and his positions on colonial domination, armed struggle, and internationalism, and his distaste for nationalist elites, struck many a chord throughout the Third World as well as in the United States among an emerging generation of Black Power advocates who arose in the shadow and aftermath of Malcolm X. For not only did the nascent Black Panther Party gain influence and inspiration from Stokely Carmichael's call for "Black Power," but as the analogies to the Third World and colonialism continued to be used as a lens to interpret Black suffering in the United States, the Black Panther Party became heavily influenced by the internationalism of Malcolm X, Kwame Nkrumah, Mao Tse-tung, Che Guevara, and Fidel Castro. But it was Frantz Fanon's ideas in particular that the Black Panther Party crafted into its vision for Black liberation.

As Kathleen Cleaver wrote, in the view of the Black Panther Party, Black peoples in the United States were "analogous to colonized people," leading Eldridge Cleaver to frame their condition in the United States in such a way that whites were the "mother country" and Black peoples were "the colony" and victims of "community imperialism." As a result of this view, Fanon's analysis of the colonial situation and his solutions for eradicating it had a profound effect on adherents to Black Power in the United States. In particular, Fanon's analysis of the segregation inherent between colonizer and native in colonial space echoed the conditions of Black peoples in the United States, segregated as they were in ghettos throughout the country. For Fanon, the colonial world was a segregated one based on race, a world in which the "cause is the consequence, you are rich because you are white, you are white because you are rich."[1]

More pointed, though, was Fanon's prescription for ending colonial domination. For Fanon, violence was inherent and endemic to the whole colonial project of control, so much so that, for Fanon, the native would have to reclaim violence to reclaim her dignity. As anticolonial insurrection raged throughout the world, Fanon's articulation of the poetics of violence seemed to give ethical and existential sanction to that rebellion, suggesting even that these insurgencies were part of a broader revolutionary movement overtaking Europe and the United States.

Along with Vietnam, Cuba, and the Congo, the Algerian resistance to French colonialism, and the work of Fanon, was brought into the orbit of Black and Third World consciousness throughout the 1950s and 1960s and into the early 1970s in a variety of different ways and by a broad cross section of activists, critics, artists, and others. During and immediately after its defeat of the French and the signing of the Évian Accords that formally ended the war in 1962, Algeria offered ideological, material, and diplomatic support to a broad range of national liberation

1. Daulatzai, *Black Star, Crescent Moon,* 51.

struggles, guerilla wars, and insurrections throughout the Third World and among Black activists and artists in the United States. In fact, Algiers would become a crossroads and meeting ground for radicals from throughout the world; as revolutionary writer and thinker Amilcar Cabral said, "pick up a pen and take note: the Muslims make the pilgrimage to Mecca, the Christians to the Vatican and the national liberation movements to Algiers!"[2]

Though Algeria would play a more prominent and visible role within Black Power in the late 1960s and early 1970s, the earlier Algerian struggle against the French had already resonated within Black political culture. In fact, Hoyt Fuller, famed editor of the *Negro Digest* (and later *Black World*), traveled to Algeria in the late 1950s and said, after his visit to the Casbah in Algiers—the center for the insurgency against the French—that Algerians and Black peoples in the United States were "fighting the same war." Harold Cruse, whose influential writings in the early 1960s made him a prominent figure within Black radical circles, had also spent time in Algeria, during World War II, and according to Cynthia Young, Cruse's shift to the radical Left occurred after his time in Algeria and his experiences witnessing the colonial relationship between the French and the Algerians.[3]

In addition, William Gardner Smith's 1963 novel *The Stone Face* explores the experiences of Simeon Brown, a Black man who escapes Jim Crow segregation and the racism of the United States and lands in Paris. Initially naive about France and believing it to be a race-free utopia, Brown soon comes to realize the racist treatment given to Algerians in France. *The Stone Face* seeks to reimagine Algerians in France as Blacks in the United

---

2. Olivier Hadouchi, "'African Culture Will Be Revolutionary or Will Not Be': William Klein's Film of the First Pan-African Festival of Algiers (1969)," *Third Text* 25, no. 1 (2011): 117.

3. Ibid. See also Cynthia A. Young, *Soul Power: Culture, Radicalism, and the Making of a U.S. Third World Left* (Durham, N.C.: Duke University Press, 2006).

States and, in doing so, positions U.S. Blacks in Paris as honorary whites. Smith uses the infamous October 1961 Papon Massacre of Algerians in Paris, which he had witnessed firsthand, to highlight Brown's decision to defiantly support the Algerians against French colonial violence, only to return to the United States to struggle on behalf of Black peoples there, to whom he now refers as "American Algerians."

James Baldwin also commented on Algeria and France's brutal colonial war. On his many trips to Paris, Baldwin discussed the existential crises that he grappled with as a Black man who was nonetheless seen as an American in France, a colonial power. He often made reference to the violent mistreatment of Algerians in Paris, the fact that they were rounded up, tortured, and put into camps outside the city, and he discussed Algerians disappearing, being killed, and being thrown into the river Seine in the infamous Papon Massacre in October 1961 in Paris. Baldwin would write, "Algeria was French only insofar as French power had decreed it to be French. It existed on the European map only insofar as European power had placed it there. It is power, not justice, which keeps rearranging the map, and the Algerians were not fighting the French for justice but for the power to determine their own destinies."[4]

In addition, when Ahmed Ben Bella, the iconic first president of Algeria, made a visit to the United States, it was headline news in numerous Black papers, including the Nation of Islam's *Muhammad Speaks*. But it was in the *New York Times* that his now famous sit-down with Martin Luther King Jr. took place. Ben Bella, King said, "believed that there was a direct relationship between the injustices of colonialism and the injustices of segregation," and King agreed that these struggles, both in the United States and abroad, were "part of a larger worldwide struggle" to end the racisms of colonialism and Jim Crow violence. King

4. James Baldwin, *No Name in the Street* (1972; repr., New York: Vintage Books, 2007), 44.

would go on to write a piece titled "My Talk with Ben Bella" in the prominent Black newspaper the *New York Amsterdam News,* that "the battle of Algerians against colonialism and the battle of the Negro against segregation is a common struggle."[5]

Malcolm X would also reference the Algerian resistance several times, whether it was in discussing his travel there, his meetings with Ahmed Ben Bella, or his famous speech "The Message to the Grassroots." The most poignant reference was made in 1964 at the Militant Labor Forum in New York, when Malcolm drew connections between Algiers, Harlem, and other Black ghettos in the United States:

> Algeria was a police state. Any occupied territory is a police state; and that is what Harlem is. Harlem is a police state, the police in Harlem, their presence is like occupation forces, like an occupying army. . . . The same conditions that prevailed in Algeria that forced the people, the noble people of Algeria, to resort to terrorist-type tactics that were necessary to get the monkey off their backs, those same conditions prevail today in America in every Negro community.[6]

Beyond the Black liberation struggles in the United States, Algeria was deeply inspired by Fidel Castro's revolution, and Cuba had quickly become a springboard for anti-imperial struggle, as Castro and Che Guevara sought to export revolution throughout the world, sending guerilla expeditions to Haiti, the Dominican Republic, Guatemala, Panama, and, later, Mozambique, Ethiopia, and Angola, among other nations. During its liberation war with France, Algeria imagined itself as the "Cuba of Africa," supporting nationalist struggles throughout the continent in the spirit of internationalism that was emblematic of the moment. With the cooperation of Ghana and Guinea, where the Algerians had

5. Martin Luther King Jr., quoted in Daulatzai, *Black Star, Crescent Moon,* 55.
6. Malcolm X, quoted ibid.

opened diplomatic offices, the FLN was active in providing a broad range of support to various African movements despite not having gained their own independence. Speaking as part of the Algerian delegation to Ghana, Fanon said, "Africa is at war with colonialism and she is impatient! . . . In our fight for freedom we should embark on plans effective enough to touch the pulse of the imperialists—by force of action and indeed violence."[7]

In building upon the international solidarities and global Third Worldism of the time, Fanon would write in *El Moudjahid,* the official organ of the FLN of which he was a part, that Algeria "must return to the Sahara its historic role as the link between Black Africa and North Africa."[8] By 1960, as its own liberation war was unfolding, Algeria provided material, diplomatic, and political support to various national liberation struggles throughout the African continent, including in Cameroon, the Congo, Senegal, Ivory Coast, Mali, Morocco, Tunisia, and Niger, while also forging alliances with rebel groups in Kenya, Rhodesia (now Zimbabwe), Angola, and apartheid South Africa. Within a year, Algerian training camps in Morocco, Tunisia, and Mali were a meeting ground for an eclectic group of guerillas and revolutionaries fighting against colonial domination, as Algeria sought to create a pan-African radicalism alongside Nkrumah, Touré, and others—a project that would continue to take shape after Algerian independence in 1962.[9]

Prior to his imprisonment, Nelson Mandela would study guerilla warfare and train with Algerian FLN fighters after denouncing nonviolence in the fight against the apartheid regime in South Africa. Che Guevara, the Bolivian revolutionary and global icon of anti-imperialism, addressed a gathering in Algiers, saying that

7. Frantz Fanon, quoted in Jeffrey James Byrne, *Mecca of Revolution: Algeria, Decolonization, and the Third World Order* (New York: Oxford University Press, 2016), 70.

8. Ibid.

9. Ibid.

"few settings from which to make this declaration are as symbolic as Algiers, one of the most heroic capitals of freedom. May the magnificent Algerian people—schooled as few others in sufferings for independence, under the decisive leadership of its party, headed by our dear compañero Ahmed Ben Bella—serve as an inspiration to us in this fight without quarter against world imperialism."[10]

Later, Kwame Nkrumah's Organization of African Unity declared Algeria to be the home to the first Pan-African Cultural Festival, which was to take place in 1969. Brilliantly captured by William Klein's documentary *The Pan-African Festival of Algiers* (1969), the gathering hosted hundreds of delegates and representatives from more than thirty newly independent African countries as well as from several countries then experiencing liberation struggles, including the People's Movement for the Liberation of Angola, the African Party for the Independence of Guinea and Cape Verde, the South West Africa People's Organization representing Namibia, the Mozambique Liberation Front, the African National Congress of South Africa, and the Black Panther Party from the United States. Fanon's ideas in *Wretched of the Earth* became the ideological backdrop to the festival, and in particular, his discussion on the role of culture in the creation of a new subjectivity distinct from Europe resonated deeply with those in attendance, as the festival's mantra became "African culture will be revolutionary or will not be!"

The festival included radical Black artists from the United States, such as poet Haki Madhubuti (Don Lee), jazz musician Archie Shepp, singer Nina Simone, Black Panther minister of culture Emory Douglas, and various other writers, artists, painters, and musicians from throughout the diaspora. Black Power expat Stokely Carmichael and his wife, Miriam Makeba, who was a singer and exiled from South Africa, were also attendees at the festival, which also became the moment when Eldridge Cleaver

10. Daulatzai, *Black Star, Crescent Moon,* 52.

revealed that Algeria had been his home in exile from U.S. persecution. William Klein's moving documentary *Eldridge Cleaver, Black Panther* (1970) captures the wanderings of Cleaver around Algiers as well as his encounters with numerous revolutionaries from around the world, providing a glimpse into the crossroads that Algeria had become for radicals and insurgents from Palestine, Vietnam, Brazil, the United States, Canada, and various African liberation movements. In fact, Algiers had become the site of the first International Section of the Black Panther Party and was used as a platform to link Black liberation struggles in the United States with other Third World liberation struggles around the world. Referred to by Kathleen Cleaver as the "Embassy of the American Revolution," the International Section lasted roughly four years, until about 1973, and ended mainly because of increasing instability in Algeria. Throughout its existence, though, the International Section provided a space for the Black Panther Party to seek the international support of other Third World revolutionaries and movements for the Black revolution taking place in the United States, much in the way that Malcolm had at the Organization of African Unity in Cairo a few years earlier.[11]

The anti-imperial militancy that characterized a broad range of struggles throughout the world drew tremendous inspiration from the Algerian liberation war and its radical theorist Frantz Fanon. The urgency of the moment demanded new transnational alliances as a bulwark against the revanchist posture of Europe and the United States, which sought to tighten their grips on the Global South. And while the realm of politics was its most obvious manifestation, the realms of art, culture, and particularly cinema also erupted with this insurgent ethos.

11. Ibid., 53.

The Camera as Gun

AS DECOLONIZATION SWEPT THE GLOBE and national liberation movements gained traction, artists, writers, intellectuals, activists, and others sought to define new nation-states in relationship to both their colonial past and their hopeful future. While discourses and debates occurred about national identity and the formation of a national culture, filmmakers, intellectuals, and artists saw art and culture as central tools to be used in shaping a revolutionary consciousness and challenging imperial and colonial orthodoxies. Whether it was the OSPAAAL in Havana, with its political graphic artwork; or the journal *Lotus* in Beirut, which was part of the Afro-Asian Writers Collective; or the Black Arts Movement in the United States, the movement known as Third Cinema had arguably the most enduring impact.

Emerging initially out of Brazil, Argentina, and Cuba and spreading throughout Africa and Asia as well, Third Cinema arose not just as an alternative but also as a challenge to dominant cinematic practice, whether it was the First Cinema, which was embodied in Hollywood, the commercial industrial cinemas in Europe and the Third World; or the Second Cinema, which was the experimental and art house cinemas of Europe and the United States. Taking various forms, Third Cinema's films have been grand epics, pseudo-documentaries, avant-garde expression, and social realism, and initially its main impetus was to complement the national struggle by heightening a revolutionary ethos around national identity and highlighting the residues of colonial power and the continued repression of minorities, women, and the poor within the nation itself. Seeking to create alternative visions of the past, present, and future, Third Cinema blended genre, aesthetics, and visual stylistics not solely for the purposes of artistic excellence but also to mobilize popular people's movements within and across borders.

Third Cinema comprises a vast array of films and documentaries, including films from western Asia (the Middle East), South America, and the African continent, including Henry Barakat's *A Man in Our House* (1961), Nelson Pereira dos Santos's *Barren Lives* (1963), Ousmane Sembene's *Black Girl* (1966), Tomás Gutiérrez Alea's *Memories of Underdevelopment* (1968) and *The Last Supper* (1976), Patricio Guzmán's *Battle of Chile* (1975), Mohammad Lakhdar-Hamina's *Chronicle of the Years of Embers* (1975), and numerous others. Many of the films narrate national liberation struggles, express the complexities of nation building, and also seek to close the gap between artists and the people by creating dialogue through a cinematic practice that engaged popular struggles.

Concerned with decolonization and cultural struggle, the seminal texts within Third Cinema were, not surprisingly, deeply influenced by the work of Frantz Fanon, in particular his book *The Wretched of the Earth*. His ideas on the formation of national culture, the role of armed struggle, and the creation of revolutionary consciousness were seen not only in the writings that formed the foundation of Third Cinema but also in the seminal films that came to define the movement as their artists and writers sought to bridge the gap between radical artistic practice and militant anti-imperialism.

Glauber Rocha's "The Aesthetics of Hunger" lays claim to a terrain cultivated by Fanon and his militant anticolonialism. For Rocha, cinema is a weapon that reveals what colonial power conceals; borrowing heavily from Fanon, colonial control involves a violent encounter, and redemptive violence on the part of the colonized is the "moment when the colonizer becomes aware of the existence of the colonized." For Rocha, the new cinema of the Third World would "reveal that violence is normal behavior for the starving" and that "the aesthetics of violence are revolutionary rather than primitive." While Rocha used Fanon as a means to give aesthetic dimension to Third Cinema, Fernando Solanas and Octavio Getino employed Fanon to give literal force to Third World film, opening their treatise with an epigram of Fanon: "We must discuss, we must invent." With this, they laid claim to a terrain where anti-imperialist cinema would fundamentally challenge the political and economic order that made Third Cinema a necessity in the first place. Teshome Gabriel's "Towards a Critical Theory of Third World Films" uses Fanon's analysis of the three stages of national culture to argue that Fanon's final "combative phase" defines Third Cinema praxis.

Fanon's influence was seen in a number of Third Cinema films as well, including Solanas and Getino's *The Hour of the Furnaces* (1968), which explicitly quotes Fanon, and Rocha's *Black God, White Devil* (1964), which reflects Rocha's "aesthetic of hunger" and mobilizes Fanon's ideas on revolutionary violence. In addition, Sembene's *Xala* (1975) embodies Fanon's penetrating criticism of the corrupt nationalist bourgeoisie. Although these filmmakers and numerous others embraced Fanon's ideas, no film is more closely associated with Fanon than Pontecorvo's 1966 film *The Battle of Algiers*.[1]

1. Daulatzai, *Black Star, Crescent Moon*.

Taking Aim: Shooting the Revolution

THE BATTLE OF ALGIERS would win numerous awards worldwide and was nominated for many others, including winning the prestigious Golden Lion Award at its debut at the Venice Film Festival in 1966, where the French delegation walked out of the award ceremony in protest. It was also nominated for an Oscar in 1967 for Best Foreign Film and again in 1969 for Best Director and Best Screenplay, and it would win the 1967 award for Best Director in Italy, Best Film in Cuba in 1967 in a *Cine* magazine poll of critics, a Periodistas Cinematográficos de México (PECIME) award among Mexican film critics, and the Kinema Junpo Award for Best Foreign Film in Japan in 1968.

David Forgacs has written about the production history of the film and details the central role that Saadi Yacef had in its making. Yacef had been the military commander for the FLN of the Autonomous Zone of Algiers during the years (1954–57) on which the film centered, and he wanted to see the Algerian nationalist struggle brought to the screen. Yacef not only acted in the film (playing Djafar, a character based on his own role in the war) but also coproduced the film as part of his Casbah Films entity. In addition, it was his own memoir (*Souvenirs of the Battle of Algiers*) that he had written while in a French prison that would form the basis of the final script. After the war was over, Yacef had written a treatment with French filmmaker René Vautier and went to Italy to find a director. Italy at that time was the largest producer of films in Europe and had a respected and even lauded recent history of neorealist films. Yacef had approached Luchino Visconti but could not come to an agreement, and so he met with Gillo Pontecorvo, a former member of the Italian Communist Party who had been part of the Italian Resistance. Pontecorvo had directed *Kapo* (1960) and had already been thinking about a film about the Algerian War of Independence, having written a script for it called *Para* that he had hoped would star Paul Newman as an American journalist covering the war. For Yacef, Pontecorvo's script was problematic because it centered on the Europeans and their perspective, and for Pontecorvo, Yacef's version was too celebratory of the FLN. Pontecorvo and his partner Franco Solinas agreed to write a new treatment based on Yacef's memoir and also to travel to Algeria, where Yacef would introduce them to those who fought and see firsthand the impact of French colonialism and the war had on everyday Algerians and the fabric of Algerian society.[1]

Pontecorvo and Solinas would complete the script, and with a relatively modest budget of eight hundred thousand dollars, shooting began in July 1965 and ended in December of that year. *The Battle of Algiers* was a joint venture between Yacef's Casbah Films and Italy's Igor Films, having received not only support from Italian financiers but also funding from private sources through Casbah Films as well as Algerian state support (which included access to locations and the use of extras, uniforms, and military equipment such as tanks and guns). For Yacef, who was the mastermind behind the film, this kind of coproduction and financing structure would expand the audience and market for the film, giving it international distribution, including to European art house cinemas and to the United States. Though elements of

1. David Forgacs, "Italians in Algiers," *Interventions: International Journal of Postcolonial Studies* 9, no. 3 (2007): 350–64.

its institutional and production history suggest a mixed inheritance of European and Algerian support, *The Battle of Algiers* remains a hallmark of Third Cinema. Despite its hybrid history, the film maintained the radical liberationist thrust of Third Cinema, while it leveraged its European support to reach a broader international audience.

Employing a docudrama style that blurred the line between fiction and documentary, the film reenacted the actual Battle of Algiers of 1954–57, powerfully magnifying the tension for the viewer through a heightened sense of realism that was a result of several formal and aesthetic choices, including the use of handheld cameras and black-and-white film (when it could have used color); its shooting in actual locales where skirmishes and bombs were placed; and its deployment of voice-overs, communiqués, and press conferences, which added to its documentary and newsreel aesthetic. In fact, the sense of realism was so high, its immediacy felt so viscerally, that the producers were forced to place a title card at the beginning of the film for American audiences that said "not one foot of newsreel has been used in this re-enactment of the Battle of Algiers."

In addition, because the revolution had just ended three years prior to shooting and was fresh in the collective memory of Algerians, the use of nonprofessional actors (with the exception of Jean Martin, who played Colonel Matthieu) was also a powerful device, as the actual participants in the national struggle were a central part of the cast and did not even have to *act* but only be themselves, including Brahim Hadjadj, who played Ali La Pointe, and Yacef, who played Djafar (a character patterned after himself). This choice, as well as filming in locations where fighting and bombing had actually taken place—both in Algiers and more particularly in the Casbah—as well as the use of actual French people still living in Algiers, furthered the immediacy and realism that Third Cinema so poetically sought to achieve.[2]

2. Daulatzai, *Black Star, Crescent Moon.*

More important was that the film challenged colonial representations of Otherness by revealing the complexity of Muslim and Arab lives. No longer were the Third World, Muslims, or any non-European subjects of empire simply set pieces for white colonial fantasy, servants to white authority, or backgrounds to stories about white anxieties. This wasn't the exotic backdrop to a tangled French romance or the heroic workings of a European protagonist pitted against "swarthy" natives in a languid desert of palm trees with lazy camels. In *The Battle of Algiers,* the Muslims had agency—limited, but agency nonetheless—that expressed itself in a demand for self-determination against those who sought to control their destinies. And unlike the cinemas of empire that centered English, French, and other European languages, *The Battle of Algiers* utilized and centered the Arabic language, giving the Algerian characters linguistic integrity and an authenticity that had up until then been denied.

But not just that. In amplifying the voices of Algerian resistance to colonial oppression, the film broke from conventional Hollywood and First Cinema practice by not centering the use of an individual protagonist who forces audience identification with that individual. Instead, the film privileges a larger collective as the protagonist—the Algerian people. In this way, the film doesn't just challenge dominant cinematic modes. It also suggests that social change and the engines of history are the product not of individuals but of collectives, be they communities or even countries. Though Ali La Pointe is one of many recurrent characters, and it is his capture around which the narrative arc is structured, the film shows that even after his death, the Algerian resistance to French colonial violence continued unabated.

Though the film has been praised as being balanced, it's clear that its sympathies lie with the Algerians. The use of musical score, close-ups, and long takes underscores the film's leanings, and maybe its most powerful impact could be felt in how the film created an empathy and identification with the Algerian rebels, whether it was with Ali La Pointe, the women moving through the checkpoints, or the Algerian people as a whole. In this way, what *The Battle of Algiers* did was close the gap between the screen and the streets, suggesting through its aesthetic choices that to identify with the Algerians on-screen would force spectators to fundamentally reconsider, and even question, dominant mainstream ideas about power and history circulating in the streets. This was the charge—and the burden—of Third Cinema: to turn viewers into active spectators who would become witnesses and, ultimately, rebels.

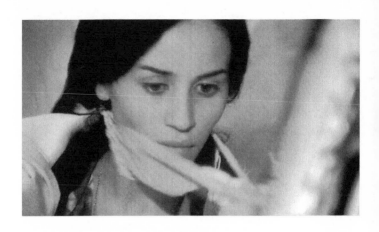

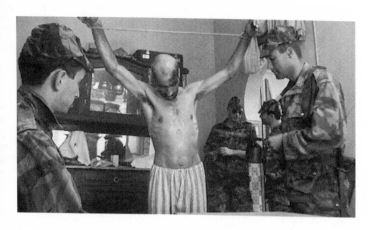

The Battle of Everywhere

WHILE THE ROOTS OF THE FILM lie in the historical and geographic specificity of the Algerian War of Independence, as well as in the political, artistic, and aesthetic contexts of decolonization, anti-imperial militancy, and Third Cinema, *The Battle of Algiers* traveled and, in some ways, became a nomadic text that found a home throughout the world. But the routes it traveled reveal a larger story about how freedom dreams were shared and how the networks of repression sought to crush popular people's struggles against the legacies of colonial and imperial rule.

As leftist and anticolonial insurgencies erupted around the globe in the 1950s, 1960s, and 1970s during the era of decolonization, Mary-Monique Robin has documented the profound influence that the so-called French School of counterinsurgency—which was forged out of the Algerian War—has had throughout the world. The French trained a broad array of repressive forces and client regimes, including Portuguese colonial forces in Angola and Mozambique, Belgian soldiers seeking to maintain control of the Congo, Iranian security officials working for the U.S.-backed Shah to quell Iranian self-determination, white South Africans seeking to maintain apartheid, U.S. military officials in their brutal war in Vietnam, and comprador Latin American military dictatorships targeting leftists and dissenters under the auspices of the CIA-backed Operation Condor.

The exportation of the French School of counterinsurgency helped to shape Operation Condor, which overthrew democratically elected president Salvador Allende of Chile in 1973 and would be part of a larger campaign that coordinated intelligence activity between the military dictatorships of Chile, Brazil, Uruguay, Argentina, Paraguay, and Bolivia. As part of the coordination throughout the Southern Cone, these states exchanged information on government opponents, which led to their assassination, detention, torture, and disappearance. As Robin details, through training received by French military officials, "the techniques used in the Battle of Algiers were carried out on a continental level with bi-national, even multinational, death squads" to strengthen Condor.[1]

In fact, *The Battle of Algiers* was used as a training tool for Latin American security officials at the International Policy Academy in Washington, D.C., and was also screened at the School of Naval Mechanics in Buenos Aires in 1967 during a series of lectures on counterinsurgency by the exiled French general Jean Gardes, who was part of the renegade, pro-settler Organisation de l'armée secrète (Organization of the Secret Army), which wanted to maintain French control of Algeria, opposed any kind of truce, and even targeted French officials and citizens for assassination, including an attempt on President Charles de Gaulle. In preparation for what would become known as the Dirty Wars in the face of a Marxist uprising in Argentina—where tens of thousands of dissidents disappeared—one of the trainees in attendance said, "They showed us the film to prepare us for a very different kind of war very different from the regular war we had entered the Navy School for. They were preparing us for police missions against

---

1. Marie-Monique Robin, "Counterinsurgency and Torture: Exporting Torture Tactics from Indochina and Algeria to Latin America," in *Torture: Does It Make Us Safer? Is It Ever OK? A Human Rights Perspective,* ed. Kenneth Roth and Minky Worden (New York: New Press, 2005), 53.

a civilian population, who became our new enemy."[2] The final Argentinean dictator of the Dirty Wars, General Bignone, later said that "we learned everything from the French: the squaring of territory, the importance of intelligence in this kind of war, interrogation methods. Our model was the Battle of Algiers."[3] In fact, the film was banned in Brazil during military rule (1964–85) for fear that victims of the security forces would recognize that French techniques of search, arrest, and torture depicted in the film could galvanize the Brazilian masses.[4]

The Battle of Algiers screened in Uruguay in 1968, where more than twenty-five thousand people viewed it after one month in the capital city of Montevideo. But it was abruptly pulled from the theaters, and instead the film was shown to the Uruguayan military for training purposes to stem the tide of a nascent leftist uprising by Tupamaros rebels. As writer Alvar de la Llosa has written, "if most of the public identified with one of the two halves of the film, with the combatants and their inflexible aspiration for liberation, now we come to discover that their enemies, the forces of colonial repression, also had their supporters." Llosa would go on to say that the film was pulled perhaps because "the techniques of urban guerrilla fighting had to be exclusive to the military institutions and not be disclosed to the public. Through this film, Uruguay became aware of the existence of numerous Colonel Matthieus within their armed forces." Llosa continued by adding that "from its prohibition, and at the risk of those responsible, none of the 25,000 spectators who were able see the *Battle of Algiers* cannot say they did not cross-check the lesson of the film with their own, immediate reality." Seeing it as an omen that would lead to the U.S.-backed overthrow of President

2. Thomas Riegler, "'The Battle of Algiers': Blueprint for Revolution/Counterrevolution?," *Resistance Studies Magazine,* no. 3 (2008): 58.

3. Robin, "Counterinsurgency and Torture," 50.

4. Riegler, "Battle of Algiers."

Salvador Allende of Chile on September 11, 1973, and unleash a reign of state terror throughout South America, Llosa went on to say that "the banning of *The Battle of Algiers* is but a harbinger of future times, it is evidence that the organization that will explode five years later is already developing, the option of military governments and application of state terrorism to an unprecedented scale in the Southern Cone, starting from September 1973."[5]

Farther north, *The Battle of Algiers* had also shown at the 1966 Acapulco Film Festival in Mexico and won the PECIME award. But, in 1967, the year before the infamous massacre at Tlatelolco, *The Battle of Algiers* was mysteriously pulled from the Cine Las Americas theaters after a record-breaking two-week run of sold-out shows. The film's popularity and its immediate removal would prove to be an omen, as the mounting tensions of the student movement culminated in the massacre at Tlatelolco, where hundreds were killed and many more were injured, jailed, and disappeared. This was ten days before the 1968 Olympics in Mexico City, in which the global upheaval of 1968 would be immortalized in the image of John Carlos and Tommie Smith raising a Black fist after wining medals at the Olympic Games. In a series of repressive measures instituted by the government, the Dirty Wars led to the disappearance and repression of many of the Mexican Left throughout the 1970s, including a professor who would flee to the mountains and reemerge as Subcomandante Marcos, spokesman for the Zapatista Army of National Liberation (EZLN), a rebel group that would shock the world and galvanize the global Left when it emerged in Chiapas to protest the North Atlantic Free Trade Agreement (NAFTA) in 1994.

But despite this response in many parts of Latin America, *The Battle of Algiers* was celebrated in Cuba, having won Best Film from *Cine* magazine in 1967. As the founding home of the Tricontinental, Cuba had become the hub for radical Third World

5. Alvar Alvar De la Llosa, "1968 En America Latina: Aparicion de Nuevos Actores," *Historia Actual Online*, no. 19 (2009): 115.

politics. The revolutionary government of Fidel Castro had become an inspiration throughout the Global South, providing ideological, diplomatic, and even military support to various national liberation struggles. Castro also understood the centrality of art in creating a national revolutionary culture, and so he funded a range of different organizations and institutions. Included in these state-sponsored initiatives was the political graphic art collective OSPAAAL, which created solidarity poster art with other liberation struggles around the world, and Instituto Cubano del Arte e Industria Cinematográficos, which trained emergent filmmakers and was instrumental in creating a vibrant film culture in Cuba that created landmark films, including *Memories of Underdevelopment* (1968), *El Otro Francisco* (1974), and *La Ultima Cena* (1976), to name a few.

Not surprisingly, Cuba would be a destination spot for revolutionaries and cultural warriors from around the globe. Christopher Hitchens, the darling of the New Left in Britain who would later betray his social justice ideals and become a warmonger and imperial loyalist in the post-9/11 era, relays that he saw *The Battle of Algiers* in Cuba in 1968 as part of a gathering of internationalists. This took place soon after the assassination of Che Guevara, the Tet Offensive in Vietnam, and the Cuban-supported Angolan resistance against Portuguese colonialism, and Hitchens was "mesmerized," as the film "looked and felt like revolutionary reality projected straight onto the screen."[6]

Across the Atlantic, the screening of the film in France has also been fraught and controversial, with the film being shown on French television for the first time in 2004. While there have been competing claims about whether the film was officially banned or censored for a period of time, Benjamin Stora claims

6. Christopher Hitchens, "Guerrillas in the Mist: Why the War in Iraq Is Nothing Like The Battle of Algiers," *Slate,* January 2, 2004. http://www.slate.com/articles/news_and_politics/fighting_words/2004/01/guerrillas_in_the_mist.html.

that many films about the Algerian War were in fact officially censored by the French government, including René Vautier's *L'Algérie en Flammes* (1958), Claude Autant-Lara's *Tu ne Tueras Point* (*Thou Shalt Not Kill*; 1961), Jean-Luc Godard's *Le Petit Soldat* (*The Little Soldier*; 1963), and Jacques Panijel's *Octobre à Paris* (1961), among others.[7]

But despite the censorship of these films, the controversy and fury unleashed by *The Battle of Algiers* were unprecedented. Since being awarded the Golden Lion after debuting at the Venice Film Festival, where the French delegation walked out in protest, French film reviews of the time had been overwhelmingly negative. And when it came to the film being shown in France, as one observer noted, "of course some people will say what about free speech? Shouldn't art be allowed to express all opinions? Well, in short, no. No decent Frenchman can accept a film that is a slur on his country."[8]

Though the film did not receive an official approval from the French government to screen until 1970, the film did screen unofficially at the Studio Luxembourg in Paris during the infamous and volatile month of May 1968. But despite this screening, subsequent showings of the film were met with threats of violence as well as actual bombings and vandalism from right-wing groups, French military veteran organizations, and *pied noirs* (French settlers), some of which led to the cancellation of screenings of the film. As Steven Whitfield notes, Pontecorvo himself coordinated with various youth organizations, as well as mobilizing public support from directors such as Louis Malle, to offset the reaction to the film, but to no avail. In fact, when three different Paris theaters scheduled openings of the film for July 1970, they were forced to cancel the screenings because of threats to the theater owners and their

---

7. Benjamin Stora, "Still Fighting: The Battle of Algiers, Censorship, and the 'Memory Wars,'" trans. Mary Stevens, *Interventions: International Journal of Postcolonial Studies* 9, no. 3 (2007): 365–70.

   8. Ibid., 368.

families by veteran groups and settler associations.[9] In September 1970, the owner of a theater in Saint-Étienne that screened the film received several anonymous phone calls before a bomb exploded nearby, while members of another right-wing group called Action Française disrupted screenings and threw ink and eggs at the screen. But despite these widespread incidences, many flocked to the theater, and over a four-month period beginning in October 1971, the film was shown to almost 150,000 people in Paris.[10] But during this period, violence continued to mark the opening of the film in October 1971 in the Latin Quarter at the Studio Saint-Severin, where conflicts and clashes between left- and right-wing groups were common, which led the owner to stop publicizing the screenings and to show the film secretly. In fact, the same theater screened *The Battle of Algiers* almost ten years later and was the target of two Molotov cocktails for showing the film, while roughly twenty men clashed with police.[11]

The film would premier at the London Film Festival in 1966 and would screen in Edinburgh, Scotland, in 1967, but it was also screened by both the British military and the IRA in their pitched battles against each other over British control of Northern Ireland. Even Pontecorvo's home country was hostile to the film. In Rome, the film was shown in July 1972, and right-wing youths attacked the audience with knives and chains. In West Germany, *The Battle of Algiers* was a favorite of Andreas Baader, the leader of the Baader–Meinhoff Group. Also known as the Red Army Faction, they were West Germany's most notorious underground guerilla group in the 1970s, comprising

---

9. "Violence Marks 'Algiers' Opening in Paris Cinema," *Variety,* November 3, 1971, 22.

10. Patricia Caille, "The Illegitimate Legitimacy of The Battle of Algiers in French Film Culture," *Interventions: International Journal of Postcolonial Studies* 9, no. 3 (2007): 371–88.

11. Stephen J. Whitfield, "Cine Qua Non: The Political Import and Impact of The Battle of Algiers," *LISA: Litteratures, histoire des Idees, Images et Societes du monde Anglophone* 10, no. 1 (2012): 249–70.

youths who had modeled their own guerilla actions against the German state based on those in the film.[12]

In the United States, well before the Pentagon screening of the film after the 2003 invasion of Iraq, both the FBI and U.S. Army intelligence operatives in 1970 also screened the film to try to silence domestic and global threats to U.S. power. These screenings took place at the height of the FBI's vicious Counterintelligence Program (COINTELPRO), which included the destabilization of leftist groups in the United States through the use of targeted assassination, disinformation campaigns, and false arrests and the imprisonment of Black Panther Party members, in particular.

As the war was raging in Vietnam, and Vietnam's National Liberation Front rebels were defeating the U.S. imperial machine, Operation Phoenix, which began in 1967 in Saigon, was part of the larger U.S. strategy for the "pacification of Vietnam." Robin details that Colonel Carl Bernard and Colonel John Johns were both stationed at the notorious Special Warfare Center in Fort Bragg, North Carolina, and were close associates of the notorious French colonel Aussaresses, who was a central figure in the torture and disappearance of thousands of Algerians during the war. Bernard and Johns would train U.S. military officials in French counterinsurgency in the 1960s, including torture, and Bernard would say that Operation Phoenix "was a copy, in every respect, of the Battle of Algiers."[13]

But while the security state was screening the film, *The Battle of Algiers* was also embraced by a range of different leftist groups in the United States, where it was a favorite among the Weather Underground and required viewing for the Black Panther Party, whose liberationist politics were linked to the anticolonial Third Worldism of Vietnam, Palestine, Cuba, and elsewhere. A *Time* magazine article at the time would write that young leftists in the United States were in admiration of the rebels in

---

12. Riegler, "Battle of Algiers."
13. Robin, "Counterinsurgency and Torture," 52.

the film, seeing them as "examples of glamorous, if not always successful revolutionaries," modeling themselves and filtering their struggles through the Algerians. The article would go on to say that "cops in San Francisco and New York both say that the movie *The Battle of Algiers* influenced much of the bombing surge. It centers on the moral dilemma of killing innocent people in the cause of revolution."[14] Emblematic of the debates and tensions that it would raise between the revolutionary Left and the more liberal cadres around the question of armed struggle, nonviolent folk singer and antiwar activist Joan Baez weighed in on the film as well: "There were people in this country who saw it as a handbook for violent revolution. But what I saw in it was an insistence that, in their terms, the most revolutionary act anyone can perform is to be able to blow up a roomful of people after having seen children in it."[15]

The film would screen at the New York Film Festival in September 1967, just after massive riots in Newark, New Jersey, and Detroit had rocked the country. As the winds of Black Power began to gust, fanning the flames of urban unrest, *Newsweek* magazine reported, "Many young Negroes cheered or laughed knowingly at each terrorist attack on the French, as if *The Battle of Algiers* were a textbook and prophecy of urban guerrilla warfare to come."[16] Three years later, at a screening of the film at the Thalia on the Upper West Side, the *New York Times* reported that there was "laughter and applause when bombs planted by Algerian women destroyed restaurants frequented by the French,"[17] and "at one point a cry of 'the United States is next' rang through the small movie house."[18]

---

14. Ibid., 55.

15. Joan Baez, quoted in Michael T. Kaufman, "Algerian Rebels in Movie Cheered," *New York Times,* August 22, 1970.

16. Riegler, "Battle of Algiers," 54.

17. J. Hoberman, "Revolution Now (and Then)!," *American Prospect,* December 15, 2003, http://prospect.org/article/revolution-now-and-then.

18. Kaufman, "Algerian Rebels in Movie Cheered."

The Battle of Algiers would open in Los Angeles as part of the New York Film Festival/West series on April 12, 1968, the week following the assassination of Martin Luther King Jr., which was clearly tied to his outspoken critiques of American imperialism in Vietnam and his linking of the war to domestic racism and economic inequality—a profound shift in his politics that was more aligned with the radical internationalist politics of Malcolm X and the burgeoning Black Power movement. *The Battle of Algiers* opened the festival, which included films that dealt with the wars in Algeria and Vietnam, including Chris Marker's *Le Joli Mai* (1963) as well as *Far from Vietnam* (1967), a film Marker produced and initiated that included the work of six directors (including, among others, Jean-Luc Godard, Agnes Varda, Alain Resnais, and William Klein), who "wanted to affirm, by the exercise of their craft, their solidarity with the Vietnamese people in struggle against aggression."[19] During its run, *The Battle of Algiers* broke box-office records in Los Angeles, including a screening where "a group of Black Panthers shows up one night, followed by a group of L.A.P.D. officers the next night."[20]

In Chicago, *The Battle of Algiers* opened at the 3 Penny Cinema on May 29, 1968, just three months before the historic Democratic National Convention took place there, an event marked by massive protests and riots, including the deployment of twelve thousand police officers and more than fifteen thousand state and federal troops to try to quell the uprising. Known as the Battle of Michigan Avenue, the protests and riots marked a turning point in the American political landscape and revealed the deep fissures between the traditional liberals and a younger, revolutionary Left over the Vietnam War and domestic racism. The film was part of the revolutionary culture overtaking

19. "Far from Vietnam," http://icarusfilms.com/new2013/far.html.
20. Greg Laemmle, "Laemmle through the Decades: 1938–2008 ~ 70 Years in 7 Days," http://www.laemmle.com/films/7640.

American society, and as a reviewer said, "Algeria and Alabama aren't that far apart."[21]

The riots resulted in the infamous Chicago Eight trial (later called the Chicago Seven), which charged members of the Black Panther Party, Students for a Democratic Society, and the Youth International Party with conspiracy and incitement to riot at the Democratic National Convention. Black Panther cofounder Bobby Seale was one of the original eight charged, who also included Tom Hayden, Rennie Davis, and Abbie Hoffman. The defendants repeatedly vocalized their discontent, at different points wearing American and Vietnamese Communist Party flags, and also judges robes, only to then take them off and walk over them in a show of performative courtroom theater. But as the only nonwhite defendant, Seale was bound with chains and gagged in front of the jury for the remainder of the trial for his demand to represent himself and for his courtroom outbursts, which provided a principled mockery of the American judicial system and critiques of American racism and militarism, which included calling the judge a "racist, a fascist and a pig."[22] He was ultimately tried separately, and though he and the others would be convicted, all the charges and sentences were ultimately overthrown. But the trial and the riots at the convention exposed the deep fissures and growing discontent in the country against domestic repression and the war in Vietnam, a rising tide of rebellion that in summer 1968 saw itself as part of the global conflagrations taking place against European and U.S. power.

The film would also be screened in 1969 at Amiri Baraka's Spirit House in Newark, New Jersey, which was the unofficial mecca of the Black Arts Movement. Formed the day after the assassination

21. Terry Clifford, "A New Theater's Gift: Violent 'Battle of Algiers,'" *Chicago Tribune,* May 30, 1968.

22. "The Case of the Defendant Who Was Bound and Gagged," http://www.crf-usa.org/bill-of-rights-in-action/bria-6-4-the-case-of-the-defendant-who-was-bound-and-gagged.

of Malcolm X, and hoping to extend the legacy of his revolutionary spirit, Amiri Baraka and others saw the Black Arts Movement as a vehicle in which poetry, literature, theater, music, and film were central to Black liberation. *The Battle of Algiers* was part of a series of films and performances that also included the 1964 film *The Dutchman* (based on Baraka's play) and the 1968 documentary on the Spirit House called *The New-Ark,* a triple feature of radical films that reflected the global sensibilities of the era.[23]

Emory Douglas, who was minister of culture for the Black Panther Party, and whose graphic artwork was the basis of the official newspaper *The Black Panther,* traveled to Algeria in 1969 and was there when Eldridge and Kathleen Cleaver emerged in Algiers for the first annual Pan-African Cultural Festival. In my conversation with Douglas, he said that, at the time, *The Battle of Algiers* was the most influential film in his life, helping to shape his artistic and political vision "because it did what I was trying to do with the Panthers—create a culture of resistance through art."[24] Not surprisingly, the Panthers would use Algiers as the site to open the first International Section of the Black Panther Party due to their admiration for the Algerian struggle, following in the footsteps of Malcolm X and James Baldwin, who also expressed their admiration for the Algerian cause. In addition, in 1970, Francee Covington would write an essay titled "Are the Revolutionary Techniques Employed in *The Battle of Algiers* Applicable in Harlem?" in the seminal anthology *The Black Woman.*

The film would also emerge as part of a much covered and controversial 1971 trial in New York City of what was known as the Panther 21, one of whom was Afeni Shakur, mother of hiphop artist Tupac Shakur, with whom she was pregnant at the

23. Whitney Strub, "Recovering the New Ark: Amiri Baraka's Lost Chronicle of Black Power in Newark, 1968," *Bright Lights Film Journal,* April 17, 2014, http://brightlightsfilm.com/recovering-new-ark-amiri -barakas-lost-chronicle-black-power-newark-1968.

24. Emory Douglas, pers. comm., February 20, 2008.

time. Charged with conspiring to explode bombs at department stores, police stations, and other locations throughout the city, the Panthers had reportedly drawn their inspiration for this plot from the film. During the trial, the prosecutor, in an attempt to sway the jury toward a conviction, showed the film to the jurors. Twice during the courtroom screening, when the French offered an Algerian rebel a fair trial, several Panthers laughed at what could only be assumed was the deep irony and parallel nature of their respective predicaments. For some of the jurors, the responses were equally striking. For juror Joe Rainato, this would be his fourth viewing. Another juror, Ben Giles, said the showing "saved me $3.50 because I was going to see it after the trial anyway,"[25] and juror Ed Kennebeck, who was now seeing the film for a third time, said, "The film did more to help me see things from the defense point of view than the D.A. suspected."[26]

Interestingly enough, *The Battle of Algiers* would become central to debates around Black representation and cinematic practice. Huey P. Newton, the Black Panther Party chairman, had embraced Mario Van Peebles's controversial 1971 film *Sweet Sweetback's Baadasssss Song* as "revolutionary" in a lengthy essay titled "He Won't Bleed Me: A Revolutionary Analysis of *Sweet Sweetback's Baadasssss Song*" and made the film required viewing for all Black Panther Party members. This added fuel to the already smoldering fire around the film. All of this ultimately led to a response by Lerone Bennett titled "Emancipation Orgasm: Sweetback in Wonderland," in which Bennett challenged Newton's assertion about *Sweetback*.

Bennett's central claim was that instead of creating imagery about Black rebellion, "it drags us into the pre-Watts days of isolated acts of resistance, conceived in confusion and executed in panic." He went on to argue that *Sweetback* "does not pose revo-

25. Catherine Breslin, "One Year Later: The Radicalization of the Panther 13 Jury," *New York Magazine*, May 29, 1972, 59.

26. J. Hoberman, "Revolution Now (and Then)!"

lutionary questions, and it does not point to revolutionary solutions. . . . It poses no questions of social structure. The movie does not show us the enemy. It does not show us the system. It doesn't show us the forces that control the black community."

And in making this point, he tellingly compared *Sweetback* the pimp to the hustler Ali La Pointe in *The Battle of Algiers*: "[Pontecorvo] shows us, Malcolm said, a hustler swinging, becoming a revolutionary and a man. He shows us that revolutions are not made in bed and that oppressed people do not triumph or love by the phallus alone." In *Sweetback,* there is no clear sense of how or when the protagonist became a revolutionary, Bennett said. "There is no such ambiguity in *The Battle of Algiers.* The male hustler in that movie turns himself inside out, like a glove, like Malcolm in fact. And like Malcolm, he confronts his former companions with the errors of their ways." Most tellingly and strikingly, Bennett raised a potential objection that is worth quoting at length:

> Some will say: "you are criticizing the man for not filming The Battle of Algiers. How could he film The Battle of Algiers when there had been no battle of Algiers in America?" But that is precisely the point. There has been a Battle of Watts in America, and a Battle of Newark, and a Battle of Detroit. A Malcolm lived in Harlem, a King in Atlanta, and Angela Davis is in a California prison. And it is impossible to make a revolutionary black film in America without taking these realities into consideration.[27]

Bennett's critique, and his use of *The Battle of Algiers* as an analogy and template for thinking through Black rebellion and Black cultural politics, reveals the deep influence that the film had on Black artists and activists. Echoing Bennett, Barbara Goldsmith wrote in a 1972 *Harper's Bazaar* piece that "blacks found an image that they could identify with in the stunning *Battle of Algiers.* Minority groups paid careful attention to this film, which pro-

27. Daulatzai, *Black Star, Crescent Moon,* 67–68.

vided the quintessential blueprint for the revolution."[28] Bennett and Goldsmith's claims came at the height of Blaxploitation cinema, which produced an oftentimes troubling negation of the more insurgent Black images that were being produced and demanded by Black Power at the time. The die had been cast, and the influence of *The Battle of Algiers* and Third Cinema more broadly found traction, not only in films like *Uptight* (1968), but also in the 1973 Ivan Dixon film *The Spook Who Sat by the Door,* which was pulled out of theaters after two weeks by the FBI because of its incendiary politics. In my conversation with him, Sam Greenlee—whose novel was the basis for Dixon's film—said of the influence of *The Battle of Algiers,* "We reached the same conclusions traveling on parallel lines."[29] The urgency of the moment would usher in a range of new voices that came to be known as the L.A. Rebellion School, who came of age at UCLA in the early to mid-1970s in the shadow of Hollywood. With films such as *Passing Through* (1977), *Killer of Sheep* (1978), and *Bush Mama* (1979), Haile Gerima, Charles Burnett, Larry Clark, Julie Dash, and others would blaze a trail of radical Black independent film deeply influenced by the movements for decolonization and Third Cinema.

The Weather Underground was also deeply influenced by the film. As white revolutionaries, the Weathermen argued in their position paper "New Left Notes" that "worldwide revolution is in progress against American imperialism by the Third World Peoples of Asia, Latin America and Africa" and that, in the United States, "this revolution is already underway on the part of the oppressed 'black colony.'" The Weathermen argued that white people had to "get on the right side" and provide material and moral support to Black and Third World struggles that will "increase the cost of empire" by forging a new front "behind enemy lines"

28. Barbara Goldsmith, "No More Workin' for the Man: Black Films Are Here to Stay," *Harper's Bazaar,* August 1972, 98.

29. Daulatzai, *Black Star, Crescent Moon,* 70.

here in the United States—much like the leftists in France who did so during the anticolonial wars in Algeria and Vietnam.[30]

In 1969, during the "Days of Rage" demonstrations in Chicago, the Weathermen imitated the sounds of the Algerian women: "we shrieked and screamed as we ran, ululating in imitation of the fighters of *The Battle of Algiers,*" said Bill Ayers. He went on to say, "I saw us become what I thought was a real battalion in a guerrilla army, and it felt for the moment like more than theatre, more than metaphor." Ayers's claim echoed Weather Underground leader Mark Rudd, who urged his compatriots to wage their own "Battle of Algiers" against the military and police establishment in the United States. Rudd claimed, "Some of the background of the Weatherman can be understood here—we look at the movie, we look at the world; a worldwide revolution is happening. A revolution is not a dinner party. Revolution happens through force of arms."[31] As could be expected, the mainstream and even liberal establishments were skeptical and even hostile to such pronouncements. Not surprisingly, the political class weighed in as well, as a Senate Report titled *The Weather Underground: Subcommittee to Investigate the Administration of the Internal Security Act and Other Internal Security Laws* included a supposed claim by a Weatherman "that radicals must abandon their comfortable, hip existence of digging *The Battle of Algiers,* the Black Panthers and other people's revolutions, smoking grass and sleeping late, and submit themselves to disciplined lives as revolutionaries."[32]

Many lived that life, including some of an estimated sixty thousand people who gathered in Harvard Square on April 15, 1970. This resulted in more than six thousand youths battling with

30. U.S. Congress, Senate, Subcommittee to Investigate the Administration of the Internal Security Act and Other Internal Security Laws of the Committee on the Judiciary, *The Weather Underground: Report,* 94th Cong., 1st sess. (1975), 9.

31. Kaufman, "Algerian Rebels in Movie Cheered."

32. U.S. Congress, Senate, *Weather Underground: Report,* 10.

some two thousand police officers in what is considered the "worst civil disturbance" in Massachusetts history. Dubbed the "Spring Offensive," the gathering was organized to protest the Vietnam War, while also demanding to free all political prisoners and to show support for the Panther 21 who were on trial in New York City. A diverse array of individuals and groups came together, including Ivy League college students, middle- and working-class groups, the Black Panther Party, the Weathermen, and coalitions such as the Vietnam Moratorium Committee and the Student Mobilization Committee. As the speakers repeatedly made the links between Vietnam and U.S. imperialism to the domestic repression of Black communities through policing, one observer noted that when the clashes ensued, the protestors "were shrieking as they had seen done in the film, *Battle of Algiers*."[33]

Arab students in the United States, who were part of the Organization of Arab Students (OAS), also mobilized as part of a broader Third World Left that was taking shape in the United States. Spurred on by the 1967 Arab–Israeli War in which Israel occupied even more Palestinian land, the OAS—which had chapters on universities throughout the United States—sought to link the struggles for Palestinian self-determination to the struggles of Black Power and other anti-imperialist groups protesting the Vietnam War, while also supporting liberation struggles in the Third World. In addition to holding teach-ins and rallies at universities, as well as organizing demonstrations at embassies and other events that hosted leaders and diplomats from Israel, the OAS organized film screenings, including co-sponsoring a festival in 1970 at Berkeley with the Liberation Support Movement, which showed films about popular struggles in Angola, Vietnam, and Palestine as well as about the Black Panther Party. Historian Pamela Pennock details these histories and writes that later in the year, the Arab students would screen *The Battle of Algiers* in

33. Lawrence J. May, "Light a Fire, Break a Window—for Peace," *Human Events*, May 2, 1970, 12.

conjunction with a film on liberation struggles in Palestine, publicizing the event with "Algiers, Vietnam, Palestine, Angola! Dig! Come and Relive the Battle!"[34]

But the activities of the OAS were not confined solely to university settings and protests at embassies. They also were deeply invested in community organizing, fund-raising, and political education. In Michigan, particularly in Detroit and Dearborn, where a large Arab diaspora population exists, OAS activists organized and built solidarity with radical Black labor groups such as the League of Revolutionary Black Workers (who were sympathetic to Palestinian self-determination) and the diverse Arab working-class immigrant communities who hailed from Lebanon, Palestine, and Yemen. As part of this, OAS activists would put together film screenings within working-class Arab neighborhoods in the early 1970s, including leftist films about Palestine and from the legendary film collective *Newsreel*. As Pennock notes, one of the films screened was *The Battle of Algiers,* and organizers were excited that many Yemeni immigrants attended, as they had been active in organizing lectures and poetry around Omani rebels fighting against the British at the time.[35]

Because of its widespread influence, *The Battle of Algiers* and the film *State of Siege* (1972) would go on to become part of a 1974 U.S. Congressional Report titled *International Terrorism.* As a clear attempt to delegitimize these films and the leftist groups in the United States who found inspiration in them, Congress also sought to challenge the truthfulness of these films so that mainstream American society, which had become increasingly skeptical of the government in the aftermath of Watergate, Vietnam, and massive social unrest, would also not find them appealing. *State of Siege* was written by Franco Solinas (who also wrote

34. Pamela Pennock, "Third World Alliances: Arab-American Activists in American Universities, 1967–1973," *Mashriq and Mahjar* 2, no. 2 (2014): 55–78.

35. Ibid.

The Battle of Algiers) and directed by Costa-Gavras, who was a leftist filmmaker also known for his 1969 film *Z*. *State of Siege*, which captured the 1970 kidnapping and execution of CIA agent Dan Mitrione by the Tupamaros, a leftist group that emerged in Uruguay in the 1960s. Mitrione was widely believed to be an advisor to the Uruguayan military on the torture and repression of the Uruguayan Left as part of the wider campaign of state terror ushered in by the U.S.-backed Operation Condor. The Congressional Report stated, "To angry, idealistic, and frustrated students, the hypnotic simplicity of the virile and romantic Tupamaros may suggest a way out of their helplessness and alienation. . . . Just as Solinas' *Battle of Algiers* was used as a training film by the Black Panthers and Weathermen, his new apology for revolutionary violence may help to encourage terror in the streets of America. If this happens, *State of Siege* will be 'playing midwife to murder,' to borrow a slogan from the Students for a Democratic Society. Hopefully the film will not have these dire consequences."[36]

Though the FBI's COINTELPRO and the revanchist policies of the United States decimated the radical Left by the late 1970s, struggles for liberation were alive and well in other parts of the world. Not only had the Vietnamese defeated the United States, ending the war in 1975, but so had many other countries gained independence from colonialism, including both Mozambique and Angola, which defeated Portuguese colonial forces.

As can be imagined, *The Battle of Algiers* was banned in both Namibia and South Africa by the apartheid regime, and it was also banned in Iran during the era of the U.S.-backed dictator Shah Pahlevi. Having been installed and backed by the United States after its successful CIA-led Operation Ajax, which overthrew the democratically elected nationalist leader Mohammad Mosaddegh in 1953, the Shah's regime banned the film from be-

36. U.S. Congress, House of Representatives, Subcommittee on the Near East and South Asia of the Committee on Foreign Affairs, *International Terrorism: Hearings,* 93rd Cong., 2nd sess. (1974), 219.

ing shown in Iran, and it wasn't screened until after the Iranian Revolution in 1979.

Echoing the trajectory of other liberation struggles throughout the Third World that, over the previous three decades, had sought to redefine national identity away from what they saw as decadent, colonial influences of the West, Iran sought to fashion a new sense of itself in the postrevolutionary period away from what Iranian intellectual Jalal Al-e-Ahmad had termed "Occidentosis" (Gharbzadegi) or "Westoxification." As film historian Hamid Naficy details, cinema was one of the main battlegrounds for this contestation across the political spectrum, from Marxists to religious figures, all of whom decried the importation of Western films. After the 1979 Revolution, Soviet and Eastern bloc films began to overtake the usual fare of American, Japanese, and Italian productions, and this influx included many films that had been banned by the Shah and that reflected the revolutionary ethos of the time, including Costa-Gavras's *Z* and *State of Siege,* Guzmán's *Battle of Chile,* and, of course, *The Battle of Algiers.* In fact, the reception to *Algiers* was so overwhelming that the film screened simultaneously in twelve theaters in Tehran and in another ten throughout the rest of the country, with one spectator noting the applause and shouts of approval coming from the audience throughout the film, while another remarked that the film was a template for "clandestine guerilla action against imperialist regimes."[37]

As Naficy details, some in the religious establishment saw value in a film like *The Battle of Algiers* because it reflected "the struggle of people oppressed by colonialism and imperialism," while others saw these films as only having "a revolutionary mask." Hojjatoleslam Ahmad Sadegi-Ardekani, a leading religious figure who oversaw the Iranian film industry in 1981, said that "acceptance of Western and Eastern films will lead us to cultural colo-

37. Hamid Naficy, *The Islamicate Period, 1978–1984,* vol. 3 of *A Social History of Iranian Cinema* (Durham, N.C.: Duke University Press, 2012), 24.

nization and economic exploitation."[38] But, according to cultural historian and political theorist Arash Davari, within months of the Revolution, the Iranian newspaper *Shurā* reported in its column *Worker's News* that *The Battle of Algiers* was screened for various labor groups and worker's collectives, including workers at a brick-burning factory in Varāmīn, laborers at the Vin Shoe Factory, and members of the national industry collective, which included workers at the United and Gabor factories.[39]

The Battle of Algiers was also embraced by the Palestine Liberation Organization (PLO) and did not play in Israel until 1983 because the FLN, which had supported the PLO, did not want the film to be screened there because of Zionist dispossession of Palestine and the occupation of their lands. But the film did play in Israel in 1983, and one reviewer noted, "Any Israeli who has served in the army in the West Bank will recognize the barbed-wire barricades, the sullen Arab faces, the body searches, the frantic chases after shadowy suspects in narrow bazaar alleys and the officers telling reporters that with just a little more time and force, the unrest will be quelled."[40]

Five years later, during the First Intifada, the film screened for weeks at the Tel Aviv Cinematheque in 1988 and sparked a firestorm of debate, as the similarities between the settler–colonial societies of French Algeria and Occupied Palestine were invoked later by Prime Minister Ariel Sharon, who would tell French president Jacques Chirac, "Mr. President, you must understand that for us here, it's like Algeria. We have no other place to go and, besides, we have no intention of leaving." These connections between the settler–colonial logics of the French in Algeria and the Zionist project in Palestine even piqued the interest of Gillo Pontecorvo. In an interview with the director, Edward

38. Ibid.

39. Arash Davari, pers. comm., January 17, 2016.

40. Marcus Eliason, "1965 Film Captivates Israelis," *Philadelphia Inquirer,* December 25, 1983.

Said, the dissident Palestinian intellectual, said that Pontecorvo had done research on a possible film on the First Intifada. Said claimed that a film on Palestinian self-determination would have been "a logical contemporary extension of the political situations represented in *The Battle of Algiers*."[41]

Jacob Norris has detailed how, during the Second Intifada, in April 2002, Israel launched Operation Defensive Shield, which resulted in the largest military campaign in the West Bank since the 1967 war. This led to the infamous massacre at the Jenin Refugee Camp, in which the Israeli Army invaded the camp and prevented any and all access, imposing a twenty-four-hour curfew that was reminiscent of the French military's invasion and cordoning off of the Casbah in Algiers during the eight-day strike of 1957. Not surprisingly, Israeli commander Moshe Tamir claimed Pontecorvo's film as a vital source of information for training his troops for Operation Defensive Shield.[42]

The Battle of Algiers was also screened in 1994 by a group of Chicano artists and activists at Regeneración/Popular Resource Center, a community center based in Los Angeles that was named after the journal started by Mexican anarchist Ricardo Flores Magón. The center, which was cofounded by Rage Against the Machine front man Zack de la Rocha and run by a collective, used film, music, theater, and performance as tools to organize and create political education around local issues and concerns impacting Chicano and Black communities in Los Angeles in the aftermath of Reagan–Bush. These included performances by Rage Against the Machine, the Watts Prophets, performance artist Guillermo Gómez-Peña, Linda Gamboa, Aztlan Underground,

41. "Gillo Pontecorvo: Dictatorship of Truth," directed by Oliver Curtis, disc 2, *The Battle of Algiers*, directed by Gillo Pontecorvo (1966; New York: The Criterion Collection, 2004), special ed. DVD.

42. Jacob Norris, "The Battle of Algiers Transposed into a Palestinian Key," *Open Democracy*, February 11, 2013, https://www.opendemocracy.net /jacob-norris/battle-of-algiers-transposed-into-palestinian-key.

and others and film screenings such as the 1973 cult classic *The Spook Who Sat by the Door* and *The Battle of Algiers*.

In my conversation with de la Rocha, he said that Regeneración screened *The Battle of Algiers* after the Zapatista uprising in Chiapas in 1994 "as a way of providing a culture of critique and to better understand Third World liberation struggles." The Zapatista rebellion occurred on January 1, 1994, the first day that the North Atlantic Free Trade Agreement was to take effect. And it captured the imagination of the Global Left in the mid- to late 1990s, as internationals flocked to Chiapas in solidarity with what was the culmination of a centuries-long struggle of indigenous peoples in the Americas against Yankee-backed repression. De la Rocha would go on to say that when he first saw the film in 1988, "*The Battle of Algiers* was central to my own political development and it led to me to better understand the connections between art and politics and the possibilities it could have in galvanizing people." De la Rocha's radical and fiery poetry would form the basis of the iconic, genre-shattering band Rage Against the Machine, who, in the 1990s, were spearheading the cultural war being waged against the ravages of the new racial capital ushered in by the Clinton presidency.

The film's influence on the band was evident, as the title of Rage's last recorded album (and arguably their best)—*The Battle of Los Angeles* (1999)—was inspired by the film. Not only that but the photos on the album sleeve included one of the band in a confined space that de la Rocha says was directly modeled after a scene in the film where Ali La Pointe and his collaborators were hiding. According to de la Rocha, "I wanted that imagery from *The Battle of Algiers* because for me the band was a musical insurgency against the industry and the system that supported it." The links to the film would carry over during the band's subsequent world tour in support of that album, as the stage design changed in each city, where a large stage backdrop would read "The Battle of London" or "The Battle of New York." The tour culminated in a DVD release of Rage's performance in Mexico titled

The Battle of Mexico City, which included the cover artwork of Mexican muralist David Alfaro Siqueiros; a documentary narrated by de la Rocha on the rise of neoliberalism and International Monetary Fund (IMF)-led globalization, the repressive U.S.-backed Mexican government, the Zapatista uprising, and the student strikes at the National Autonomous University of Mexico, which is the largest university in Latin America; and an interview with Subcomandante Marcos of the EZLN. The battle lines were drawn, and though it was a violent time, the 1990s were in some ways the calm before the 9/11 storm. Rage's body of work throughout the decade was a warning shot that also proved prophetic in the post-9/11 era, and it did so carrying with it the legacy of *The Battle of Algiers* and the radical internationalism that was its utopian demand.[43]

The nomadic nature of the film throughout the world and the archive of its traces brim with the triumph and the tragedy of popular struggles and the seemingly intractable forces that continue to shape-shift and seek the silencing and repression of these radical movements. But the film's screening at the U.S. Pentagon in the post-9/11 era is not just another episode in the longer saga that is the dynamic afterlife of the film. Instead, the fact that it was produced during the era of decolonization, and that it inspired movements of anti-imperial militancy and Black Power, worker's struggles, and student movements throughout the world, reveals that *The Battle of Algiers* continues to haunt the imperial consensus, an enduring reminder of a freedom dream not yet achieved.

43. Zack de la Rocha, pers. comm., February 2016.

Prologue

The 9/11 Present: Perpetual War and Permanent Unrest

THOUGH IT IS BOTH TROUBLING AND TELLING, the screening of the film by the Pentagon in the aftermath of 9/11 and the invasions of Iraq and Afghanistan is only the latest chapter in the after-life of *The Battle of Algiers.* In many ways, the film is a battle-ground and a microcosm of the enduring struggles between the West and the Rest, whiteness and its others. But in a post-9/11 moment, it's hard to ignore the ways in which the centrality and omnipresence of the figure of the Muslim and the "War on Terror" have not only coded and shaped every aspect of social life but have also sought to undermine the power and politics of *The Battle of Algiers.*

In many ways, the "War on Terror" has used the pretense of "antiterrorism" and the haunting figure of the Muslim to gar-ner public support and generate political will to usher in new repressive measures on a global scale. Occupying what Fanon called a "zone of non-being," the figure of the Muslim has au-thorized permanent war abroad and repression at home, the ex-pansion of police powers and the deepening of the surveillance state, the undermining of women's liberation and the criminal-ization of migrants, indefinite detention and the legitimacy of torture, the silencing of speech, and the disciplining of dissent.

But the screening of the film at the Pentagon and its use as a training tool in the "War on Terror" have—through appropriation and revisionism—sought to control the memory of *The Battle of Algiers* and have also deflected and undermined many of the urgent questions and concerns that decolonization and the Third World Project sought to address. Despite this, the *Battle of Algiers* in many ways resists this kind of imperial containment, and in nuanced and sophisticated ways, the film provides an opportunity to probe more deeply into the contemporary moment, as many of its central themes still resonate today.

Terror

In a moment of profound cinematic reversal, and one that had prophetic echoes across the Tricontinental and the landscape of Bandung, is the scene from *The Battle of Algiers* when Ben H'midi, the leader of the FLN, is captured and paraded as a spectacle in front of a preening press. Asked about his use of guerrilla war and the FLN's targeting of civilians, Ben H'midi replied, "Isn't it even more cowardly to attack defenseless villages with napalm bombs that kill thousands more? Obviously planes would make things easier for us. Give us your bombers and you can have our baskets."

Ben H'midi's and, by extension, the film's sympathetic portrayal of guerrilla warfare targeting colonial occupying forces and settler-civilians resonated across the Third World and shook the colonial and imperial foundations of international law. From France to Israel, South Africa to Brazil, the film was banned precisely because of its ethical endorsement of guerrilla war against occupying forces and repressive, Western-backed dictatorships. In profound ways, this has arguably been the central and enduring legacy of the film, inaugurating a debate within the United Nations and among political theorists and policy makers about what constitutes "terrorism" and legitimate resistance, conventional war and asymmetric guerrilla warfare.

The Battle of Algiers gave ethical sanction to armed struggle and popular resistance to colonial occupation and imperial power. But in the current "War on Terror," the ruling paradigm of "counter-terrorism" and the language and logic of "terror/-ism/-ist" have created a security logic that not only has served to delegitimize and criminalize armed struggle but also has had a profound chilling effect on speech, dissent, and other forms of political activity.

In fact, in an era of the "post-racial," the language of "terror-ism" has been used as a language of race-craft that is a twenty-first-century way of saying "savage," of rekindling in somewhat stark terms the colonial discourse of "civilization" and "savagery." As dog whistle terminology for invoking race and Otherness, the logic of "terror" (like "savage" before it) determines who is human (read: White) and who is not by excluding particular ideas, bodies, regions, and collectives from the political community of rights. As subjects who exist outside the law, Muslims, then, are not only not due protection by the law; they are also subject to the full force of the "law" and all manner of "extralegal" force (torture, invasion, warfare, drones, indefinite detention, incarceration, etc.) to protect the rights of those deemed human. By ushering in a new architecture of control, the "War on Terror" has marked "terrorism" as illegitimate speech and activity, creating a legal framework for prosecuting it, policing powers to manage it, and a military response for executing it.

This framing of Muslim being, agency, and resistance outside the bounds of the human and what is deemed legitimate political activity is central to understanding the rewriting of the film and its legacy in the post-9/11 context. The embrace of the film during its release by a broad and diverse group of radicals and revolutionaries—from the IRA to the PLO, Baader–Meinhoff to the Black Panthers, Marxists to nationalists—speaks to its universal appeal. Yes, the film stood for militancy and revolutionary action writ large, one that was only nominally about Muslims per se—as Third World decolonization and international solidarity gave *The Battle of Algiers* a more universal appeal that was so vital at the time.

But in the post-9/11 context, with the decimation of the Third World Project and also the viability and visibility of a coherent global Left, this kind of radical universality that was the film's appeal has been replaced by a more troubling and particularist reading that *The Battle of Algiers* isn't simply a film about Muslims resisting the occupation of their lands by the West (in this case, the French); it is a film that *sympathetically* portrays that resistance. But in a post-9/11 context, armed struggle—let alone resistance of *any* kind—by Muslims is seen as dangerous, as worthy of death, and is targeted by the state through legal, political, and military regimes of violence.

During decolonization, the film provided a space for the ways in which the Muslims of Algeria were an entrée into a larger panorama of anticolonial resistance. But in the lingua franca of imperial culture today, the Muslim now stands in for the limits and poverty of armed struggle and radical activity writ large. This overdetermined framing lends itself to a reading of the film where not only is the past rewritten—as Algerian resistance to French colonialism is delegitimized through the contemporary "War on Terror"—but so too is the current project of empire coded as innocent, one where there is a historical continuity between the French of yesterday and the Americans of today.

According to the Directorate for Special Operations and Low-Intensity Conflict in charge of the screening of *The Battle of Algiers* at the Pentagon in 2003, "showing the film offers historical insight into the conduct of French operations in Algeria, and was intended to prompt informative discussion of the challenges faced by the French." The Pentagon's screening signaled an attempt by the military establishment to reframe the film not as text about decolonization and anti-imperialism but instead as a manual for "how to do counterinsurgency," not only stripping the film of its radical impulses but also erasing the violent history of colonialism as the determining force for Algerian resistance. This reversal and act of appropriation not only purified the colonial past; it was also an attempt to sanitize and strip away the current moment of U.S. empire and frame contemporary Muslim struggles in Iraq, Afghanistan, Palestine, and elsewhere within the ruling paradigm of "terrorism" that has to be crushed. But this revisionism is only possible because the ideological space available to understand Muslim agency, Muslim subjectivity, and Muslim being has eroded and withered away in the post-9/11 moment, so that the very thing that made the film so groundbreaking—its ability to dignify Algerian struggles and elicit sympathy from viewers for their cause—is almost unimaginable today: a move that situates French colonialism as just, and the current U.S. imperial footprint as necessary.

Torture

The opening scene of *The Battle of Algiers* plunges the viewer into a kind of complicity. Having just finished torturing Sedek, the French now know where the last cell, which includes the elusive Ali La Pointe—is located. As the viewer, we don't witness the torture firsthand, but we *know* it happened. We are left instead with the aftermath. Much like with the torture-porn of Abu Ghraib, Bagram, Guantánamo, and other "black sites," we are also witnesses, carrying the burden of knowing.

By opening with a scene of torture, *The Battle of Algiers* presents the stark violence that has been at the heart of the colonial encounter: not just the violence of the act of torture itself—the electrical shock, the fists, the waterboarding, and the death—but also the violent conditions of colonialism that made a rebellion necessary in the first place. In fact, as Fanon has argued, violence structures the colonial encounter and the relationship between the empire and its Others, and this is brilliantly mirrored in the way the film's narrative is in fact structured by torture and colonial violence.

The film brilliantly shows Fanon's ideas about the segregation of colonial space, between "white" Algiers and the Casbah (where the Algerians were confined). Through the film, we see the barricades and the barbed wire, the checkpoints and the surveillance cameras—a space of violence where the police and the military are the enforcers of colonial authority. There is also the prison where Ali La Pointe is radicalized into political consciousness—à la Malcolm X—his eyes peering through the prison bars as a rebel is walked to the guillotine. The blade is dropped but an awareness is raised as chants of "Long Live Algeria!" and "Allah U Akbar!" echo through the prison walls. And there is the torture, shown in almost operatic and elegiac ways that, though brutal, still didn't reveal the extent of the French torture program, which included the rape and torture of Algerian women, sometimes in their own homes.

But in terms of what it does show, the sense of realism the film conveyed made it seem shocking and unbelievable. To the deniers of empire and apologists of colonialism, *The Battle of Algiers* was too real, shattering a world of white invincibility and colonial authority that Algerians and the larger Third World had so desperately sought to tear down. Maybe the film was shocking to so many because resistance to colonialism is *real* and because colonial authority and popular discourse around empire have sanitized and presented a Eurocentric world so bloodlessly, one where the flags of empires—British, French, Dutch, Italian, U.S.— fly so benevolently. The shock, then, shouldn't have been directed at the means the Algerians used to usurp and throw off the shackles of white colonial power but rather at the centuries-long violence that has been used to keep Algerians, and the larger Global South, subjugated for so long.

Despite the guerrilla actions by the Algerians in the film, the overwhelming violence throughout the history of colonialism in Algeria (1830–1962) and during the Algerian War of Independence (1954–62) was committed by the French. To establish their presence in Algeria, the French ushered in policies where mass displacement of Algerians took place as well as dispossession of the land, including the pacification of the country that led to the violent crushing of nationalist uprisings against French rule and death by famine, war, and disease. Robert Stam cites the writer Victor Hugo, who, in his book *Choses Vues,* discusses a conversation he had with a French general two decades after French colonization of Algeria began. Hugo reports that at that October 16, 1852, meeting, the general told him, "It was not rare, during the French attacks, to see soldiers throwing Algerian children out of the window onto the waiting bayonets of their fellow soldiers. They would rip the earrings off the women, along with the ears, and cut off their hands and fingers to get the rings."[1]

During the War of Independence, the French executed more than three thousand prisoners, and during which time estimates claim that twenty thousand French soldiers and upward of 1.5 million Algerians were killed.[2] The French used helicopters, tanks, and planes; airstrikes on civilians; and advanced rifles and grenades as well as the creation of internment camps and the destruction of thousands of villages, not to mention systematic and routinized forms of torture. But we have to understand violence in more systemic forms as well that don't include only the bomb, the gun, or the tool of torture. Violence is also the exploitation of the country, the seizing of land and its resources, the legal and political codes that enforced the destruction of Algerian social life, and the wealth accumulation that structured the asymmetries of political, diplomatic, and military power. And then there is the epistemic violence that imposed French history and language within schools, and other institutions of the country that marginalized the varieties of Algerian social and cultural lives to be expressed and to flourish. Colonialism is indeed a violent phenomenon, and we have to be attuned to the myriad forms this violence takes and through which it is routinized and normalized with-

1. Robert Stam, "Fanon, Algeria, and the Cinema: The Politics of Identification," in *Postcoloniality, Multiculturalism, and Transnational Media,* ed. Ella Shohat and Robert Stam (New Brunswick, N.J.: Rutgers University Press, 2003), 22–23.

2. Ibid., 22.

in the everyday functioning of empire. If we do, then we cannot create a moral or ethical equivalence between French violence to crush the national liberation struggle and Algerian resistance to French colonialism. To do so is not just ahistorical; it's unethical.

On the question of torture, many scholars have pointed out that for the colonial and imperial powers, torture is not an aberration but rather is central to the foundation and maintenance of modern liberal democracy. In France during the Algerian War of Independence, the specter of torture marked the French empire. Two books, Henri Alleg's *The Question* (1958) and *The Gangrene* (1959), were banned by the French government. Alleg was a French Communist, and counter to the official French Communist Party position, which backed colonial control of Algeria, Alleg advocated through his journalism for Algerian independence. His memoir—*The Question*—was based on his arrest and torture by the French and became a best seller, though it was soon censored by the French government as the Algerian independence struggle intensified. Another searing indictment was the book *The Gangrene,* which struck a deep chord and was immediately censored, as the French government confiscated all copies by pulling them from the shelves and storming the publishing house. The book told the true story of four Algerians living in Paris who were arrested and brutally tortured by French police for their suspected ties to the Algerian independence struggle. The book revealed the widespread use of torture against Algerians taking place in France, although no French official was ever held responsible. And then, of course, there are the cases of two Algerian women, Djamila Bouhired and Djamila Boupacha. Bouhired, who was captured and tortured by the French, was depicted in *The Battle of Algiers* as one of the three women bombers, while also being the subject of the 1958 Youssef Chahine film *Jamila, the Algerian.* Boupacha's case became a cause célèbre among the intellectual and artistic Left, as figures such as Simone de Beauvoir, Henri Alleg, and Pablo Picasso rallied to her support after her torture and rape while in prison brought attention to the widespread systematic use of sexual violence by the French.[3]

In the film, when he is asked about torture at the press conference, Matthieu claims that "the word torture does not appear in our orders," a claim that was eerily echoed by U.S. president George W. Bush when the Abu Ghraib tortures were revealed, saying "we do not torture" and instead preferring the Orwellian euphemism "enhanced interrogation techniques." Like Bush, Matthieu also said that he had to "interrogate," but he went on to say, "And that's where we find ourselves hindered by a conspiracy of laws and regulations that continue to operate as if Algiers were a holiday resort and not a battleground. . . . Should we remain in Algeria? If you answer yes, then you must accept all the necessary consequences."

This sentiment was echoed by a U.S. solider when the tortures at Abu Ghraib prison in Iraq were first revealed: "It's a little like the French colonel in *The Battle of Algiers.* You're all complaining about the tactics I'm using to win the war, but that's what I'm doing, winning the war."[4] Not surprisingly, it's no coincidence that the blueprint for U.S. counterinsurgency in Iraq and Afghanistan—the Petraeus Doctrine—is deeply influenced by and borrows heavily from the work of French military specialist David Galula, whose *Counterinsurgency Warfare* and *Pacification in Algeria* are central to U.S. policy in the "War on Terror."

But despite its glorification in films like *Zero Dark Thirty* (2012), in the *Senate Intelligence Committee Report* on Torture, and in the self-righteous "debate" that ensued between those who claimed that "to torture is un-American and betrays our values"

3. See Henri Alleg, *The Question* (1958; repr., Lincoln, Neb.: University of Nebraska Press, 2006), and *The Gangrene,* trans. Robert Silvers (New York: Lyle Stuart, 1960).

4. Thomas E. Ricks, "Commander Punished as Army Probes Detainee Treatment," *Washington Post,* April 5, 2004, http://www.washingtonpost.com/wp-dyn/articles/A50227-2004Apr4_2.html.

and that "torture is a necessary evil to stop an imminent attack," torture is normalized as an expedient means by which Western democracies constitute and imagine themselves. In fact, torture has been central to U.S. national security, including its use against Black prisoners domestically as a means of social control. According to historian Alfred McCoy, "at the deepest level, the abuse[s] at Abu Ghraib, Guantanamo, and Kabul are manifestations of a long history of a distinctive U.S. covert warfare doctrine developed since World War II."[5] McCoy continues by claiming that the U.S. "torture paradigm can be seen in the recurrence of the same techniques used by American and allied security agencies in Vietnam during the 1960's, Central America in the 1980's and Afghanistan and Iraq since 2001. Across the span of three continents and four decades, there is a striking similarity in U.S. torture techniques—from the C.I.A.'s original Kubark interrogation manual, to the agency's 1983 Honduras training book, all the way to Ricardo Sanchez's 2003 orders for interrogation in Iraq."[6]

In *The Battle of Algiers,* Matthieu is not presented as evil. Instead, his dispassionate persona and rational, matter-of-fact style suggest that the violence from colonialism and empire is not simply the product of evil men with bad morals and intentions but the product of the workings of a system in which many are complicit. Hanna Arendt referred to this as the "banality of evil" in reference to Nazi Germany, and Matthieu's comments at his impromptu press conference regarding the need to accept "all necessary consequences" can be seen in a similar light, as he points out the hypocrisies of even the liberal establishment, which criticized the means and methods of war. Matthieu unwittingly held up a mirror to both the Left and the Right of French society, and his comments can also be read as a cautionary tale to future empires, like the United States today, where a series of

5. Alfred W. McCoy, *A Question of Torture: CIA Interrogation, from the Cold War to the War on Terror* (New York: Metropolitan Books, 2006), 7.
6. Ibid., 12.

similar ethical questions might be posed: "If you and your citizens want that lifestyle of comfort, of excess and pleasure, then just know what it takes to get it, and don't complain or rely on liberal platitudes about how 'America has lost its way.' That oil? Those cell phones and laptops? The clothes on your backs? Or even the land you live on? If you value this lifestyle, then don't complain about the methods needed to maintain it." The implications are stunning and disturbing, penetrating and indicting.

Gender

Central to the structuring of the Muslim outside the category of the human is the role of gender. In a powerful scene, *The Battle of Algiers* challenges the racial and gendered logics of colonialism by subverting the "discourse of the veil." The film's portrayal of Zohra, Hassiba, and Djamila, three women who "looked" as though they had embraced European values of modernity—only to pass through a checkpoint without being searched and then successfully plant bombs among French settler-civilians—revealed the veil, and, more important, Western feminist values, to be overdetermined and, ultimately, a ruse.

Deeply reflective of what has been called feminist Orientalism, or imperial feminism, First Lady Laura Bush addressed the nation soon after the invasion of Afghanistan, saying, "The fight against terrorism is also a fight for the rights and dignity of women." Her comments about the connections between women's rights and war are a contemporary expression of a centuries-long project of Western colonialism and intervention that privileges not just white feminism but also Western models of liberation. But as Leila Ahmed, Lila Abu-Lughod, and others have pointed out, contemporary debates about women's rights, freedom, and equality can be traced back to earlier colonial and missionary ideas and rhetorics about Muslim women.

In the current post-9/11 context, the figure of the Muslim woman has been used to make claims about Islam and Muslim societies as the sole and exclusive sites of patriarchy and misogyny, as the question of women's rights has become the legitimizing discourse for the claims that Islam and Muslim societies are fundamentally illiberal and antimodern. In fact, the figure of the Muslim woman has been central to expanding the logic of the "War on Terror" by further racializing Muslim communities and marshaling support from both feminists and conservatives, liberals and leftists, for military expansion, imperial war, and nation building. As scholar Sherene Razack has argued, the imperiled Muslim woman has become an archetype, one who must be rescued from genital mutilation, forced marriage, and the veil and saved in the West, becoming "a rationale for engaging in the surveillance and disciplining of the Muslim man and of Muslim communities."[7]

Echoing Fanon's famous—and controversial—essay "Algeria Unveiled," the film suggests that the conventional Western logic that the veil is a sign of repression and that its removal means freedom is troubled. In the film, scenes depicted Muslim women with the veil as "dangerous," for they could hide weapons beneath their clothes. But in the scene where the women "de-veil," the film suggests that Muslim women without the veil, looking "Western," are potentially even more dangerous, for they passed as "civilized" and "modern," no longer enslaved by their traditions and their men, as the colonial logic would dictate. Muslim women now had agency, could speak, and could act on their own accord. And in the turning point of the film, the Muslim woman expresses her "agency"—limited though it is—but not as the French would have liked. Instead, it is her resemblance *to* the French, or her "aspirations" to be "modern," that grants her access to "choice." And because she looks that way, still appealing to the (white) male gaze, she is able to pass through the checkpoint and plant the bombs in the cafés and airport terminals. In this radical moment of subversion, the film suggests the poverty in the

7. Sherene Razack, *Casting Out: The Eviction of Muslims from Western Law and Politics* (Toronto: University of Toronto Press, 2008), 142.

"discourse of the veil" and the colonial logic of "saving Muslim women." For to de-veil and to "look" European or modern is a ruse, for it can seemingly suggest that an embrace of European or Western values about feminism is where "freedom" resides. But as numerous feminist scholars and the film itself suggest, it's the subjectivities and the embodiment of them that ultimately provide value and meaning and that must be understood in a wider social and political context.

These claims about the veil as oppressive not only present the West as egalitarian and free from patriarchy but also ignore the work of Muslim women both in the West and in Muslim societies struggling and fighting against the structural forces that shape women's inequality. In doing so, imperial feminism conveniently masks how patriarchy is actually operating and rooted throughout the world, including in the West. For it is often the case that when the patriarchy and misogyny of Muslims is brought up, the women of the West, and their male accomplices, turn away from domination at home, ignoring the structures that subjugate women in the West, while also ignoring how patriarchy in Muslim societies, and the Global South more broadly, is rooted and maintained by institutions and state-building initiatives that are tied to larger political and economic questions about IMF and neoliberal policy, war and poverty, that are a direct product of the legacies of colonialism and the violent continuation of Western intervention. As Charles Hirschkind and Saba Mahmood ask, "why were conditions of war, militarization, and starvation considered to be less injurious to women than the lack of education, employment, and, most notably, Western dress styles?"[8]

It is this continued legacy of colonialism today and the unfinished project of decolonization that continue to haunt the present and make *The Battle of Algiers* an urgent and prescient film.

8. Charles Hirschkind and Saba Mahmood, "Feminism, the Taliban, and Politics of Counter-Insurgency," *Anthropological Quarterly* 75, no. 2 (2002): 345.

Though *The Battle of Algiers* captured the demand for national liberation, one of the more striking moments in the film was the rooftop scene between Ali La Pointe and FLN leader Ben H'midi, who tells the younger Ali, "It's hard enough to start a revolution, even harder to sustain it, and hardest of all to win it. But it's only afterwards, once we've won, that the real difficulties begin." Filmed in 1965 just after the military overthrow of Ahmed Ben Bella that brought Houari Boumediene to power and placed Ben Bella under house arrest, this scene is not only a reflection of the internecine fighting of the FLN three years after the end of the war but also a larger cautionary tale about the difficulties of nation building in the postindependence period for the broader Global South. Fanon warned us about this in *The Wretched of the Earth,* where he expressed a deep skepticism of nationalist elites whom he felt, after independence, would betray the popular will and the project of liberation by continuing to do Europe's bidding by proxy.

This is why the film is significant today: not because it seemingly captures "terrorists at work," and thereby provides a kind of voyeurism or even "teaching tool" in the post-9/11 climate, but because it helps to reveal the continuities between the era of decolonization and the present. That is, the "War on Terror" is not a rupture per se but is rather another chapter in an ongoing campaign of counterinsurgency against the Global South, one that of course started centuries ago with colonialism proper, continued with neocolonial control through Bretton Woods, the IMF and Third World debt, extended with the Cold War, deepened with "globalization" and neoliberalism, and continues today under the rubric of the "War on Terror." *The Battle of Algiers,* then, is relevant precisely because the very issues the film raised about self-determination have yet to be fully contended with— decolonization being an unfinished project that continues to haunt the imperial present.

The film was released in the crucible of decolonization and at the high point of Third Worldism and internationalism. Third Cinema became a means to reframe subjectivity so that it was the Algerians whom audiences were to identify with and whose cause they were to sympathize with. But now, in a post-9/11 context, viewers are caught, confused maybe, and even resistant. For to now identify with Muslims who are planting bombs and targeting occupying forces seems like an endorsement of 9/11 and "terrorism." But maybe this ambiguity and confusion are productive and hold the possibility that some fundamental questions about the role of power and history, and how these forces unfold in the present, can be raised.

In seeking to close the gap between the screen and the streets, *The Battle of Algiers* suggests that to identify with the Algerians in the theater should force a fundamental reconsideration and questioning of dominant ideas in society and the public at large. And if that's the case, then one might be more likely to identify with a Palestinian, Afghan, or anyone else on the receiving end of state violence and then maybe challenge or question the "War on Terror" and the logic of empire. So that instead of asking "why are we *there* (Iraq, Afghanistan, etc.)?" and "do they really hate our freedom?" we might reply that "maybe they simply want their own." This was the impulse of the film—one that still brims with the radical possibility that it might turn citizens into skeptics, or, better yet, take Fanon's dictum that "every spectator is a coward or a traitor" and force one to choose.

As much as the film was about the Algerian War for Independence, it was also prophetically a warning and a call to arms. Its stark depiction of people struggling to overcome was poignant and an exemplar. Though *The Battle of Algiers* saw a resurgence in the post-9/11 moment, the film carries with it a kind of poetic inscrutability, an illicit and clandestine impulse that resists being neutralized within the amalgam of imperial static. Yes, the Pentagon has sought to rewrite its meaning and significance. But that they viewed it, probed it, and examined it also suggests that they *fear it*. Ali La Pointe is still alive. So is Hassiba and the young boy Omar. That is why they torture. Invade. Drone. Imprison. And kill. They are on the hunt. But it's we—the hungry—who will win.

Acknowledgments

Thanks to Danielle Kasprzak at University of Minnesota Press and the reviewers for all your support. Huge shout-out to the brilliant Eszter Zimanyi for your invaluable research skills! Thanks to Kevin Durst and Zaphira Yacef of Casbah Films, and of course to Saadi Yacef, Gillo Pontecorvo, and Franco Solinas, for a masterpiece. To all those in the Casbahs worldwide: stay chisel and know that our time will come. To my cipher—Oscar Michel, Zack de la Rocha, Aamer Rahman, Arash Davari, Yousef Baker, Arash Saedinia, Junaid Rana, and Adilifu Nama—steel sharpen steel! Love to my family for everything. And to the moon and star: keep shining your light!

Sohail Daulatzai is the author of *Black Star, Crescent Moon: The Muslim International and Black Freedom beyond America,* coeditor of *Born to Use Mics: Reading Nas's Illmatic,* and curator and editor of *Return of the Mecca: The Art of Islam and Hip-Hop.* He teaches in the Department of Film and Media Studies, the Department of African American Studies, and the program in Global Middle East Studies at the University of California, Irvine.

Made in the USA
San Bernardino, CA
14 June 2017